AF484016

Feeding Frenzy

Feeding Frenzy

Matthew Petchinsky

Feeding Frenzy: Graboid-Inspired Recipes
By: Matthew Petchinsky

Disclaimer:

This is an independent, fan-created work inspired by the *Tremors* film series. It is not affiliated with, endorsed by, or connected to Universal Pictures, Stampede Entertainment, or any other rights holders of the *Tremors* franchise. All trademarks, characters, creatures, and related elements of *Tremors* remain the property of their respective owners. The recipes and content in this book are original creations intended for entertainment and culinary enjoyment only.

Introduction: Unearthing the Culinary World of Graboids

The vast deserts of Perfection Valley have been home to a creature as elusive as it is iconic: the Graboid. Known to fans of the *Tremors* franchise as the subterranean behemoth with an insatiable appetite, the Graboid has become a symbol of survival, ingenuity, and primal hunger. First unearthed in 1990, these monstrous predators captured imaginations with their terrifying speed, razor-sharp senses, and sheer determination to consume anything in their path. Yet, behind their fearsome reputation lies an undeniable inspiration for this culinary adventure.

In this unique cookbook, we delve into the lore of the Graboid and explore how their voracious appetite inspired a collection of hearty, bold, and underground flavors. Much like the Graboids themselves, these recipes are not for the faint of heart—they demand courage, creativity, and an appetite for adventure. This introduction serves as your gateway to a gastronomic journey that celebrates both the ferocity of the Graboid and the rich, earthy essence of its underground habitat.

The Graboid's Appetite: A Culinary Muse

The Graboid's eating habits are legendary, consuming livestock, machinery, and even the occasional unlucky human. But their appetite speaks to something deeper—an unyielding connection to the earth itself. They are creatures of the underground, navigating hidden worlds where roots, tubers, and minerals abound. This cookbook draws inspiration from that primal connection, using bold ingredients and grounded flavors to craft dishes that embody the Graboid's essence.

From rich stews and hearty casseroles to root-based sides and earthy desserts, the recipes within are a tribute to the Graboid's unrelenting hunger. Each dish is designed to be as filling and satisfying as the creature's infamous meals—minus the perilous chase, of course.

Culinary Themes: Hearty, Bold, and Underground

The recipes in this collection are guided by three central culinary themes:

1. **Hearty:** Graboids don't nibble; they devour. The dishes in this book reflect that approach, offering hearty, stick-to-your-ribs meals that satisfy even the hungriest diners. Think rich braises, rustic breads, and robust flavors that linger long after the last bite.
2. **Bold:** Inspired by the Graboid's untamed spirit, these recipes feature bold flavors that aren't afraid to stand out. Smoky spices, intense umami, and unexpected ingredient pairings take center stage, transforming each dish into a fearless flavor journey.
3. **Underground:** The subterranean world is alive with culinary potential. This cookbook emphasizes ingredients that come from beneath the surface, such as root vegetables, tubers, mushrooms, and other earthy delights. These ingredients not only honor the Graboid's underground habitat but also add depth and complexity to the recipes.

Tips for Sourcing Ingredients and Equipment

Cooking with the spirit of the Graboid requires both resourcefulness and preparation. Here are some tips to ensure success in your culinary journey:

1. **Ingredients:**
   - **Root Vegetables and Tubers:** Staples like potatoes, sweet potatoes, carrots, parsnips, and turnips are essential. Look for locally grown, organic options to capture their full earthy flavor.
   - **Mushrooms:** From cremini and shiitake to wild varieties like chanterelles, mushrooms bring an underground essence to many dishes. Visit farmers' markets or specialty stores for the freshest selection.
   - **Hearty Proteins:** Graboids don't shy away from meat, and neither should you. Opt for robust cuts like brisket, lamb shank, or pork shoulder, which can stand up to bold flavors and long cooking times.
   - **Spices and Herbs:** Smoky paprika, cumin, garlic, and thyme are your allies in creating bold, memorable flavors. Experiment with spice blends to capture the untamed spirit of the Graboid.
2. **Equipment:**
   - **Cast Iron Cookware:** Whether for slow-cooked stews or seared meats, a sturdy cast iron skillet or Dutch oven is invaluable.
   - **Earthy Presentation:** Wooden boards, ceramic bowls, and rustic platters enhance the visual appeal of your underground-inspired dishes.
   - **Basic Foraging Gear:** For the adventurous cook, consider trying your hand at foraging for mushrooms or wild herbs—just be sure to research thoroughly and forage responsibly.

With this introduction, you're ready to embrace the bold spirit of the Graboid and let its legendary appetite guide you through a one-of-a-kind culinary experience. Let's dig in!

Chapter 1: Digging In – Appetizers That Bite

Appetizers set the stage for any great meal, and when crafting dishes inspired by the ferocious Graboids, you'll want starters that pack a punch. This chapter, aptly named "Digging In," features bold, flavor-packed appetizers that not only tantalize the taste buds but also reflect the untamed, earthy essence of the subterranean hunters themselves. Each recipe is designed to deliver a satisfying kick—whether through spice, texture, or a combination of both.

Spicy Graboid Jalapeño Poppers

These fiery delights are the perfect tribute to the Graboid's ferocious nature. Each jalapeño is stuffed with a creamy, smoky filling, wrapped in bacon, and baked to golden perfection. The spice is bold, the flavors are deep, and the texture delivers the crunch of a bite you'll never forget.

Ingredients:

- 12 large jalapeños
- 8 oz cream cheese, softened
- 1 cup shredded cheddar cheese
- ½ cup cooked and crumbled bacon
- 2 green onions, finely chopped
- 1 tsp smoked paprika
- 1 tsp garlic powder
- 12 strips of bacon (optional, for wrapping)
- Toothpicks

Instructions:

1. **Prepare the Jalapeños:**
   - Preheat your oven to 375°F (190°C).
   - Slice each jalapeño in half lengthwise and remove the seeds and membranes (leave some seeds for extra heat if desired).
   - Set the cleaned halves aside on a lined baking sheet.
2. **Make the Filling:**
   - In a mixing bowl, combine the cream cheese, cheddar cheese, crumbled bacon, green onions, smoked paprika, and garlic powder. Mix until well combined.
3. **Stuff the Peppers:**
   - Use a spoon to fill each jalapeño half generously with the cheese mixture.
4. **Optional Bacon Wrapping:**
   - If you'd like to add an extra layer of indulgence, wrap each stuffed jalapeño with a strip of bacon, securing it with a toothpick.
5. **Bake to Perfection:**
   - Arrange the poppers on the baking sheet and bake for 20–25 minutes, or until the bacon is crispy and the cheese filling is bubbling.
6. **Serve and Enjoy:**
   - Let the poppers cool slightly before serving, then dig in and feel the bite!

These Spicy Graboid Jalapeño Poppers are a crowd-pleaser at any gathering, offering just the right amount of heat to wake up the palate.

Rock-Burrowed Cheese Dip with Pretzel Rods

Like a Graboid burrowing through the earth, this gooey, decadent cheese dip is a treasure waiting to be unearthed. Served with salty pretzel rods for dipping, this appetizer combines the rich, creamy flavors of melted cheese with an earthy, smoky twist.

Ingredients:

- 2 tbsp unsalted butter
- 2 tbsp all-purpose flour
- 1 cup whole milk
- 1 cup sharp cheddar cheese, shredded
- ½ cup smoked gouda, shredded
- ¼ tsp ground mustard
- ½ tsp smoked paprika
- ½ tsp garlic powder
- 1 tbsp Worcestershire sauce
- Salt and pepper to taste
- Pretzel rods for serving

Instructions:

1. **Make the Roux:**
   - In a medium saucepan, melt the butter over medium heat. Once melted, whisk in the flour and cook for 1–2 minutes, stirring constantly, until the mixture is golden and smells nutty.
2. **Add the Milk:**
   - Slowly pour in the milk, whisking constantly to ensure no lumps form. Continue cooking and stirring until the mixture thickens, about 3–5 minutes.
3. **Melt the Cheese:**
   - Reduce the heat to low and gradually stir in the cheddar and gouda. Allow the cheeses to melt completely, creating a smooth, creamy dip.
4. **Season the Dip:**
   - Stir in the ground mustard, smoked paprika, garlic powder, Worcestershire sauce, and a pinch of salt and pepper. Taste and adjust seasoning as needed.
5. **Serve with Pretzel Rods:**
   - Pour the cheese dip into a heat-safe serving bowl and serve immediately with pretzel rods for dipping.

Optional Additions:

- For an extra "underground" flavor, stir in finely chopped mushrooms or caramelized onions.
- Add a sprinkle of crushed red pepper flakes for a spicy kick.

Bringing the Bite to Your Table

With appetizers like these, you're setting the tone for a meal full of bold, unforgettable flavors. The Spicy Graboid Jalapeño Poppers and Rock-Burrowed Cheese Dip capture the adventurous spirit of the *Tremors* franchise while offering dishes that everyone around the table can enjoy. Whether you're hosting a themed dinner party or simply diving into some hearty snacks, these recipes are guaranteed to disappear faster than a Graboid in the sand.

Chapter 2: Sand-Trap Soups and Stews

When survival in the underground world of Perfection Valley is at stake, a warm, hearty bowl of soup or stew can feel like the ultimate refuge. In this chapter, we dig deep into the comforting world of soups and stews, where bold flavors meet nourishing ingredients. Inspired by the Graboid's subterranean habitat and voracious appetite, these dishes highlight earthy vegetables, rich broths, and layers of spice that evoke the thrilling tension of the *Tremors* franchise.

Whether you're huddled up on a chilly night or preparing a meal to satisfy the hungriest of guests, these recipes promise to deliver warmth, flavor, and a sense of adventure in every spoonful.

Subterranean Sweet Potato and Lentil Soup

This hearty and nutritious soup is a tribute to the root-laden world of the Graboid. Sweet potatoes bring an earthy sweetness, while lentils provide protein-packed sustenance. Together, they create a deeply satisfying dish that feels like a comforting hug from the underground.

Ingredients:

- 2 tbsp olive oil
- 1 medium onion, diced
- 2 cloves garlic, minced
- 2 medium sweet potatoes, peeled and diced
- 1 cup red lentils, rinsed
- 1 tsp ground cumin
- 1 tsp smoked paprika
- ½ tsp ground turmeric
- 4 cups vegetable broth
- 1 cup coconut milk
- Salt and pepper to taste
- Optional toppings: fresh cilantro, a drizzle of olive oil, or a sprinkle of red chili flakes

Instructions:

1. **Sauté the Aromatics:**
   - Heat the olive oil in a large pot over medium heat. Add the onion and garlic, sautéing until soft and fragrant, about 3–5 minutes.
2. **Build the Base:**
   - Stir in the sweet potatoes, lentils, cumin, smoked paprika, and turmeric. Cook for 2–3 minutes, allowing the spices to bloom and coat the vegetables.
3. **Simmer the Soup:**
   - Pour in the vegetable broth, bringing the mixture to a boil. Reduce the heat to low, cover, and simmer for 20–25 minutes, or until the lentils and sweet potatoes are tender.
4. **Blend and Finish:**
   - Use an immersion blender to purée the soup to your desired consistency (smooth or slightly chunky). Stir in the coconut milk and season with salt and pepper to taste.
5. **Serve and Enjoy:**
   - Ladle the soup into bowls and garnish with your choice of toppings. Serve with crusty bread or crackers for an even heartier meal.

This Subterranean Sweet Potato and Lentil Soup is a perfect representation of the Graboid's connection to the earth—nourishing, bold, and grounded.

Graboid Gumbo: A Swampy Delight

Taking a detour into swampy terrain, this gumbo is as bold and untamed as a Graboid emerging from the sand. Packed with shrimp, sausage, and a medley of vegetables, this dish is simmered in a spicy, flavorful roux that captures the essence of Louisiana's culinary heritage.

Ingredients:

- ¼ cup vegetable oil
- ¼ cup all-purpose flour
- 1 medium onion, diced
- 1 green bell pepper, diced
- 2 stalks celery, diced
- 3 cloves garlic, minced
- 1 tbsp Cajun seasoning
- 1 tsp smoked paprika
- 1 tsp thyme
- 1 (14 oz) can diced tomatoes
- 6 cups chicken or seafood broth
- 1 lb andouille sausage, sliced
- 1 lb shrimp, peeled and deveined
- 1 cup okra, sliced
- 2 cups cooked white rice
- Salt, pepper, and hot sauce to taste

Instructions:

1. **Make the Roux:**
   - In a large pot, heat the vegetable oil over medium heat. Whisk in the flour and cook, stirring constantly, until the roux turns a deep brown color (about 10–15 minutes). Be patient; the depth of the roux's color is key to the gumbo's flavor.
2. **Sauté the Vegetables:**
   - Add the onion, bell pepper, celery, and garlic to the roux. Sauté for 5–7 minutes until the vegetables are softened.
3. **Season and Build the Base:**
   - Stir in the Cajun seasoning, smoked paprika, thyme, and diced tomatoes. Slowly pour in the broth, whisking to combine. Bring the mixture to a gentle boil.
4. **Add the Protein and Okra:**
   - Reduce the heat to low and add the sliced sausage and okra. Simmer for 20–25 minutes, allowing the flavors to meld.

5. **Finish with Shrimp:**
     ◦ Stir in the shrimp and cook for an additional 5 minutes, or until the shrimp are pink and cooked through. Adjust seasoning with salt, pepper, and hot sauce to taste.
6. **Serve and Enjoy:**
     ◦ Spoon the gumbo over cooked white rice and serve hot. Offer additional hot sauce on the side for those who dare to turn up the heat.

This Graboid Gumbo is a swampy, spicy delight that delivers layers of bold flavors in every bite.

The Warm Comfort of Sand-Trap Soups and Stews

Soups and stews are the ultimate expressions of comfort food, and these recipes take that comfort underground. Whether it's the earthy sweetness of the Subterranean Sweet Potato and Lentil Soup or the bold, swampy flavors of Graboid Gumbo, these dishes are guaranteed to satisfy both your hunger and your sense of adventure. They're perfect for family dinners, game nights, or themed parties celebrating the wild spirit of the *Tremors* universe.

Chapter 3: Earth-Shaking Salads

Salads may seem like a calm and collected part of any meal, but in the spirit of the *Tremors* universe, they deserve a little shake-up. This chapter explores bold and earthy salads inspired by the subterranean world of the Graboids. Packed with vibrant colors, rich textures, and robust flavors, these salads celebrate the bounty of the underground—root vegetables, hearty grains, and earthy dressings that bring the depth and character of the Graboid's habitat to your table.

From a nutrient-packed quinoa and beet salad to a zesty slaw bursting with tangy mustard flavors, these dishes prove that salads can be just as thrilling as the fiercest chase through the desert.

Burrowing Beet and Quinoa Salad

Beets, with their deep, earthy flavor and vibrant color, are the stars of this nutrient-rich salad. Paired with protein-packed quinoa, fresh herbs, and a zesty citrus dressing, this salad captures the Graboid's connection to the earth while delivering a refreshing and satisfying dish.

Ingredients:

- 1 cup quinoa, rinsed
- 2 medium beets, roasted and diced
- 1 cup baby spinach or arugula
- ¼ cup chopped fresh parsley
- ¼ cup chopped fresh mint
- ¼ cup crumbled feta cheese (optional)
- ¼ cup toasted walnuts or almonds
- Zest and juice of 1 orange
- 2 tbsp olive oil
- 1 tbsp balsamic vinegar
- Salt and pepper to taste

Instructions:

1. **Cook the Quinoa:**
   - In a medium saucepan, bring 2 cups of water to a boil. Add the rinsed quinoa, reduce the heat to low, and cover. Cook for 15 minutes, or until the water is absorbed and the quinoa is fluffy. Set aside to cool.
2. **Prepare the Beets:**
   - If not already roasted, wrap the beets in foil and roast in a 400°F (200°C) oven for 45–60 minutes, or until tender. Let cool, peel, and dice into bite-sized pieces.
3. **Make the Dressing:**
   - In a small bowl, whisk together the orange juice, zest, olive oil, and balsamic vinegar. Season with salt and pepper to taste.
4. **Assemble the Salad:**
   - In a large mixing bowl, combine the cooked quinoa, roasted beets, spinach or arugula, parsley, and mint. Toss gently to combine.
5. **Add the Toppings:**
   - Sprinkle the salad with feta cheese (if using) and toasted nuts. Drizzle with the citrus dressing and toss lightly.
6. **Serve and Enjoy:**
   - Transfer to a serving platter or individual plates and enjoy a salad that's as vibrant as it is delicious.

This Burrowing Beet and Quinoa Salad is a perfect blend of earthy, nutty, and citrusy flavors—a light but satisfying dish inspired by the Graboid's underground lair.

Root Veggie Slaw with Tangy Mustard Dressing

This slaw brings together an assortment of root vegetables in a crunchy, colorful dish that's as bold as the Graboids themselves. Tossed in a tangy mustard dressing with a hint of sweetness, this slaw pairs perfectly with heavier mains or stands on its own as a vibrant side dish.

Ingredients:

- 1 medium carrot, julienned or shredded
- 1 medium parsnip, julienned or shredded
- 1 small turnip, julienned or shredded
- ½ small red cabbage, thinly sliced
- 2 green onions, thinly sliced
- ¼ cup chopped fresh dill
- ¼ cup dried cranberries or raisins (optional)
- 2 tbsp sunflower seeds or pumpkin seeds (optional)

For the Tangy Mustard Dressing:

- 3 tbsp Dijon mustard
- 2 tbsp apple cider vinegar
- 1 tbsp honey or maple syrup
- 3 tbsp olive oil
- 1 tsp celery seed (optional)
- Salt and pepper to taste

Instructions:

1. **Prepare the Vegetables:**
   - In a large mixing bowl, combine the carrot, parsnip, turnip, red cabbage, green onions, and dill. Toss to mix evenly.
2. **Make the Dressing:**
   - In a small bowl, whisk together the Dijon mustard, apple cider vinegar, honey or maple syrup, olive oil, and celery seed (if using). Season with salt and pepper to taste.
3. **Dress the Slaw:**
   - Pour the dressing over the vegetables and toss thoroughly to coat. Adjust seasoning if needed.
4. **Add Optional Toppings:**
   - If desired, sprinkle the slaw with dried cranberries or raisins and seeds for extra texture and flavor.
5. **Serve and Enjoy:**
   - Let the slaw sit for at least 10 minutes before serving to allow the flavors to meld. Serve as a side dish or a topping for sandwiches and wraps.

This Root Veggie Slaw with Tangy Mustard Dressing is a crunchy, zesty celebration of the underground harvest, making it a fitting tribute to the Graboid's earthy roots.

The Vibrancy of Earth-Shaking Salads

Salads may live in the shadow of heartier dishes, but with these recipes, they take center stage. The Burrowing Beet and Quinoa Salad and the Root Veggie Slaw with Tangy Mustard Dressing are vibrant, bold, and packed with the kind of underground flavors that the Graboid itself would envy. Whether served as sides or light meals, these salads bring a fresh, earthy energy to your table—proving that even the humblest of dishes can deliver a seismic impact.

Chapter 4: Tremor-Worthy Tacos

When it comes to bold, handheld meals that pack a flavorful punch, tacos reign supreme. In this chapter, we dive into the subterranean culinary world of *Tremors* to create taco recipes that are as legendary as the Graboids themselves. These Tremor-Worthy Tacos bring together fresh, earthy ingredients and bold spices, offering a range of textures and flavors that evoke the wild, untamed spirit of Perfection Valley.

From crispy fish tacos with a spicy kick to deeply spiced mushroom tacos that honor the underground habitat of the Graboids, these recipes will leave your taste buds trembling with delight.

Crispy Graboid Fish Tacos

These tacos are a tribute to the Graboid's aquatic relatives, the Ass-Blasters, and their legendary appetite. Tender white fish is coated in a crispy, golden batter, paired with a tangy slaw, and topped with a spicy crema for the ultimate taco experience.

Ingredients:

For the Fish:

- 1 lb white fish fillets (e.g., cod, halibut, or tilapia)
- 1 cup all-purpose flour
- 1 tsp smoked paprika
- 1 tsp garlic powder
- ½ tsp cayenne pepper
- ½ tsp salt
- ½ cup beer or sparkling water
- Vegetable oil for frying

For the Slaw:

- 2 cups shredded cabbage (green or red)
- 1 medium carrot, julienned or shredded
- 2 tbsp chopped fresh cilantro
- 1 tbsp lime juice
- 1 tbsp mayonnaise
- Salt and pepper to taste

For the Spicy Crema:

- ½ cup sour cream or Greek yogurt
- 1 tbsp hot sauce (e.g., sriracha or chipotle)
- 1 tsp lime juice

For Assembly:

- 8 small corn or flour tortillas, warmed
- Lime wedges, for serving

Instructions:

1. **Prepare the Slaw:**
   - In a mixing bowl, combine the cabbage, carrot, cilantro, lime juice, and mayonnaise. Season with salt and pepper to taste. Cover and refrigerate until ready to use.
2. **Make the Spicy Crema:**
   - In a small bowl, mix together the sour cream, hot sauce, and lime juice. Adjust the spice level to your preference and set aside.
3. **Prepare the Batter:**
   - In a medium bowl, whisk together the flour, smoked paprika, garlic powder, cayenne pepper, and salt. Gradually add the beer or sparkling water, whisking until the batter is smooth and thick enough to coat the fish.
4. **Fry the Fish:**
   - Heat about 1 inch of vegetable oil in a deep skillet or saucepan over medium-high heat. Cut the fish into taco-sized strips, dip each piece into the batter, and fry in batches until golden and crispy, about 3–4 minutes per side. Drain on paper towels.
5. **Assemble the Tacos:**
   - Place a few pieces of fried fish on each tortilla. Top with a generous scoop of slaw and drizzle with the spicy crema. Serve with lime wedges for squeezing over the top.

These Crispy Graboid Fish Tacos are a perfect blend of crunch, tang, and heat—a taco worthy of the *Tremors* legacy.

Underground Spiced Mushroom Tacos

For a vegetarian option that's just as bold and satisfying, these mushroom tacos are a must-try. Loaded with earthy, spiced mushrooms and paired with a vibrant avocado salsa, they embody the Graboid's deep connection to the subterranean world.

Ingredients:

For the Mushrooms:

- 1 lb mixed mushrooms (e.g., cremini, shiitake, or oyster), sliced
- 2 tbsp olive oil
- 1 tsp smoked paprika
- 1 tsp cumin
- 1 tsp chili powder
- ½ tsp garlic powder
- ½ tsp salt

For the Avocado Salsa:

- 2 ripe avocados, diced
- 1 small red onion, finely chopped
- 1 medium tomato, diced
- 1 tbsp lime juice
- 1 tbsp chopped fresh cilantro
- Salt and pepper to taste

For Assembly:

- 8 small corn or flour tortillas, warmed
- Crumbled cotija cheese (optional)
- Lime wedges, for serving

Instructions:

1. **Cook the Mushrooms:**
   - Heat olive oil in a large skillet over medium-high heat. Add the sliced mushrooms and sauté until golden and tender, about 5–7 minutes.
   - Sprinkle the smoked paprika, cumin, chili powder, garlic powder, and salt over the mushrooms. Stir to coat evenly and cook for an additional 2 minutes to let the spices bloom.
2. **Prepare the Avocado Salsa:**
   - In a bowl, gently mix together the avocado, red onion, tomato, lime juice, and cilantro. Season with salt and pepper to taste.
3. **Assemble the Tacos:**
   - Spoon the spiced mushrooms onto each tortilla. Top with a scoop of avocado salsa and sprinkle with cotija cheese, if desired. Serve with lime wedges for added brightness.

These Underground Spiced Mushroom Tacos are packed with flavor, offering a satisfying bite that pays homage to the earthy depths of the Graboid's habitat.

Tacos That Shake Things Up

Tacos are a perfect canvas for creativity, and these Tremor-Worthy Tacos are no exception. Whether you're savoring the crispy, spicy flavors of the Graboid Fish Tacos or the earthy, spiced depth of the Underground Mushroom Tacos, these recipes are guaranteed to be a hit. They're ideal for game nights, themed parties, or simply spicing up your dinner table with a touch of *Tremors* magic.

Get ready to dig in—because when it comes to these tacos, the only thing more legendary than their inspiration is their flavor.

Chapter 5: Predator's Pizza

Few meals bring people together like pizza, and in the spirit of *Tremors*, this chapter dives deep into the art of crafting pizzas that are as bold and unrelenting as the Graboids themselves. Predator's Pizza features two epic creations designed to satisfy even the most ferocious appetite.

The **Deep-Dish Graboid Meat Lovers' Pizza** is a hearty, indulgent pie piled high with layers of savory meats and rich cheese, while the **Burrowed Veggie Flatbread** celebrates the underground with a medley of earthy, roasted vegetables and bold flavors. Whether you're feeding a crowd or indulging in a solo pizza adventure, these recipes are sure to shake up your kitchen and bring a slice of *Tremors*-inspired magic to the table.

Deep-Dish Graboid Meat Lovers' Pizza

This deep-dish pizza is as intense as a Graboid's appetite. With layers of savory sausage, pepperoni, bacon, and melted cheese, every bite is packed with flavor. The buttery, thick crust serves as the perfect foundation for this meat-lover's dream.

Ingredients:

For the Crust:

- 3 ½ cups all-purpose flour
- 1 tsp sugar
- 1 packet (2 ¼ tsp) active dry yeast
- 1 tsp salt
- 1 ¼ cups warm water (110°F/45°C)
- ¼ cup olive oil

For the Toppings:

- 1 cup pizza sauce
- 1 ½ cups shredded mozzarella cheese
- ½ cup cooked Italian sausage, crumbled
- ½ cup pepperoni slices
- ½ cup cooked bacon, crumbled
- ½ cup diced ham
- ¼ cup grated Parmesan cheese

Instructions:

1. **Make the Dough:**
   - In a large bowl, combine the warm water, sugar, and yeast. Let sit for 5 minutes, or until the yeast is foamy. Add the flour, salt, and olive oil, mixing until a dough forms.
   - Knead the dough on a floured surface for about 8 minutes, until smooth and elastic. Place in a lightly oiled bowl, cover, and let rise for 1 hour, or until doubled in size.
2. **Preheat and Prep:**
   - Preheat the oven to 425°F (220°C). Grease a 12-inch cast iron skillet or deep-dish pizza pan with olive oil.
3. **Shape the Crust:**
   - Punch down the dough and roll it out to fit your pan. Press the dough into the pan, ensuring it comes up the sides to form a deep-dish crust.
4. **Assemble the Pizza:**
   - Spread the pizza sauce evenly over the crust. Sprinkle half of the mozzarella cheese over the sauce. Add the Italian sausage, pepperoni, bacon, and ham in even layers. Top with the remaining mozzarella and finish with grated Parmesan.
5. **Bake to Perfection:**
   - Bake the pizza for 25–30 minutes, or until the crust is golden brown and the cheese is bubbly and slightly browned.
6. **Serve and Devour:**
   - Let the pizza cool for 5 minutes before slicing and serving. Prepare for a flavor explosion worthy of the fiercest Graboid!

Burrowed Veggie Flatbread

For a lighter, earthy take on pizza, this flatbread highlights the underground world with roasted vegetables, creamy goat cheese, and fresh herbs. The thin, crispy crust serves as the perfect canvas for these bold, subterranean flavors.

Ingredients:

For the Flatbread Base:

- 1 ½ cups all-purpose flour
- ½ tsp salt
- ½ cup water
- 2 tbsp olive oil

For the Toppings:

- 1 small sweet potato, thinly sliced
- 1 small beet, thinly sliced
- ½ cup sliced mushrooms
- ¼ cup red onion, thinly sliced
- 2 tbsp olive oil
- Salt and pepper to taste
- ½ cup crumbled goat cheese
- 1 tsp fresh thyme leaves
- 1 tbsp honey (optional)

Instructions:

1. **Make the Flatbread Dough:**
   - In a bowl, combine the flour, salt, water, and olive oil. Mix until a dough forms. Knead on a floured surface for 5 minutes, until smooth. Cover and let rest for 20 minutes.
2. **Prepare the Vegetables:**
   - Preheat the oven to 400°F (200°C). Toss the sweet potato, beet, mushrooms, and red onion with olive oil, salt, and pepper. Spread on a baking sheet and roast for 15–20 minutes, or until tender.
3. **Roll Out the Dough:**
   - Divide the dough into two portions and roll each into a thin oval or rectangle. Place on a parchment-lined baking sheet.
4. **Assemble the Flatbread:**
   - Brush the flatbread with olive oil. Arrange the roasted vegetables on top, then sprinkle with goat cheese and thyme leaves.

5. **Bake and Finish:**
   - Bake for 10–12 minutes, or until the flatbread is crispy and golden. Drizzle with honey if desired for a hint of sweetness.

6. **Serve and Enjoy:**
   - Slice and serve immediately, savoring the earthy, layered flavors of this Burrowed Veggie Flatbread.

The Bold World of Predator's Pizza

Pizza is more than a meal—it's a canvas for creativity and bold flavors. The **Deep-Dish Graboid Meat Lovers' Pizza** brings hearty, indulgent satisfaction, while the **Burrowed Veggie Flatbread** offers a fresh and earthy alternative. Together, these recipes honor the primal hunger and earthy essence of the Graboids, ensuring every bite is as exciting as an underground chase.

Whether you're feeding a family or hosting a *Tremors*-themed movie night, these pizzas are guaranteed to be the star of the show. Prepare your oven, roll out the dough, and let your inner Graboid loose—because these pizzas are worth every tremor.

Chapter 6: Above Ground Grilling

Grilling is where fire meets flavor, and it's the perfect way to channel the untamed spirit of the Graboids. In this chapter, we rise above the underground to explore the art of cooking over open flames, bringing bold, smoky flavors to the table. From succulent chicken skewers coated in a rich BBQ glaze to hearty portobello mushroom burgers packed with earthy, umami goodness, these recipes are inspired by the rugged, outdoor survival ethos of the *Tremors* universe.

Whether you're hosting a backyard cookout or enjoying a quiet evening grilling under the stars, these dishes are guaranteed to deliver a satisfying bite that echoes the wild energy of Perfection Valley.

Tremor BBQ Chicken Skewers

Juicy, flavorful, and slightly charred, these BBQ chicken skewers are a nod to the heat and thrill of a Graboid encounter. Marinated in a smoky-spiced BBQ sauce and grilled to perfection, they're ideal for any outdoor feast.

Ingredients:

For the Marinade:

- 2 lbs boneless, skinless chicken thighs, cut into bite-sized pieces
- ½ cup BBQ sauce (store-bought or homemade)
- 2 tbsp olive oil
- 1 tbsp soy sauce
- 1 tbsp honey or brown sugar
- 1 tsp smoked paprika
- 1 tsp garlic powder
- ½ tsp ground cumin
- ½ tsp chili powder

For Grilling:

- Wooden or metal skewers (soaked in water for 30 minutes if wooden)
- Extra BBQ sauce for basting

Instructions:

1. **Prepare the Marinade:**
   - In a large bowl, mix the BBQ sauce, olive oil, soy sauce, honey, smoked paprika, garlic powder, cumin, and chili powder. Add the chicken pieces and toss to coat thoroughly. Cover and refrigerate for at least 1 hour (or up to overnight) to allow the flavors to develop.
2. **Assemble the Skewers:**
   - Thread the marinated chicken onto skewers, leaving a little space between each piece for even cooking.
3. **Preheat the Grill:**
   - Heat your grill to medium-high. Lightly oil the grates to prevent sticking.
4. **Grill the Skewers:**
   - Place the skewers on the grill and cook for 10–12 minutes, turning occasionally and basting with extra BBQ sauce during the last few minutes of cooking. Ensure the chicken reaches an internal temperature of 165°F (74°C).
5. **Serve and Enjoy:**
   - Transfer the skewers to a platter and let them rest for 5 minutes before serving. Pair with coleslaw, grilled corn, or a tangy dipping sauce for a complete meal.

These Tremor BBQ Chicken Skewers are smoky, juicy, and packed with flavor—a perfect tribute to the heat of the grill and the thrill of the chase.

Graboid-Inspired Portobello Burgers

For a hearty, plant-based option, these portobello burgers are the ultimate homage to the Graboid's earthy habitat. Thick, meaty mushrooms are marinated in a savory blend of spices and grilled until tender, then topped with your favorite burger fixings for a delicious, umami-packed sandwich.

Ingredients:

For the Mushrooms:

- 4 large portobello mushroom caps, stems removed and gills scraped out
- ¼ cup balsamic vinegar
- 2 tbsp olive oil
- 1 tbsp soy sauce
- 1 tsp smoked paprika
- 1 tsp garlic powder
- ½ tsp onion powder
- ½ tsp black pepper

For Assembly:

- 4 burger buns (toasted, if desired)
- Lettuce leaves
- Sliced tomato
- Sliced red onion
- 4 slices of cheese (optional, such as Swiss, cheddar, or vegan cheese)
- Condiments (e.g., mayonnaise, mustard, or BBQ sauce)

Instructions:

1. **Prepare the Marinade:**
   - In a shallow dish, whisk together the balsamic vinegar, olive oil, soy sauce, smoked paprika, garlic powder, onion powder, and black pepper.
2. **Marinate the Mushrooms:**
   - Place the portobello caps in the dish and coat them thoroughly with the marinade. Let sit for at least 30 minutes, flipping halfway through.
3. **Preheat the Grill:**
   - Heat your grill to medium-high and lightly oil the grates.

4. **Grill the Mushrooms:**
   - Remove the mushrooms from the marinade and place them on the grill. Cook for 4–5 minutes per side, or until tender and slightly charred. If using cheese, add a slice to each mushroom during the last minute of grilling to allow it to melt.
5. **Assemble the Burgers:**
   - Spread your chosen condiments on the bottom half of each bun. Top with a lettuce leaf, a grilled mushroom cap, tomato slices, and red onion. Add the top bun and serve immediately.
6. **Serve and Enjoy:**
   - Pair these burgers with sweet potato fries, grilled veggies, or a fresh salad for a well-rounded meal.

These Graboid-Inspired Portobello Burgers are hearty, flavorful, and perfect for vegetarians or anyone craving a lighter alternative that doesn't skimp on taste.

Above Ground Grilling: Flame and Flavor

Grilling brings out the primal joy of cooking over an open flame, and these recipes elevate that experience with bold, Graboid-inspired flavors. The **Tremor BBQ Chicken Skewers** and **Graboid-Inspired Portobello Burgers** are not just meals—they're experiences that celebrate the thrill of the grill and the wild spirit of *Tremors*.

Perfect for backyard gatherings, camping trips, or themed dinners, these dishes will make you a grill master worthy of the Graboids' legendary status. Fire up your grill, embrace the heat, and let these recipes shake up your grilling game.

Chapter 7: Hearty Underground Casseroles

When it comes to comfort food, casseroles are the ultimate dish. Layered with robust flavors and hearty ingredients, they bring warmth and satisfaction to any table. In this chapter, we dive underground with casserole recipes inspired by the subterranean world of the Graboids. These **Hearty Underground Casseroles** showcase bold flavors, earthy vegetables, and rich textures, making them perfect for feeding a hungry crowd or savoring leftovers that taste even better the next day.

The **Buried Beef and Potato Bake** is a layered masterpiece of tender beef, creamy potatoes, and savory sauce, while the **Digging Deep Shepherd's Pie** reinvents a classic with an earthy twist, using a root vegetable mash for the topping. These dishes are substantial, satisfying, and unapologetically indulgent—just what you'd expect from a Graboid-inspired meal.

Buried Beef and Potato Bake

This casserole is a hearty, layered dish that combines tender beef, sliced potatoes, and a creamy sauce that bubbles to golden perfection in the oven. It's a tribute to the Graboids' underground habitat, where each layer of flavor is unearthed bite by bite.

Ingredients:

- 1 lb ground beef
- 1 medium onion, finely chopped
- 2 cloves garlic, minced
- 2 tbsp olive oil
- 1 tsp smoked paprika
- 1 tsp thyme
- ½ tsp ground cumin
- Salt and pepper to taste
- 4 large potatoes, peeled and thinly sliced
- 1 cup heavy cream
- 1 cup milk
- 2 tbsp all-purpose flour
- 1 cup shredded cheddar cheese
- ¼ cup grated Parmesan cheese
- 2 tbsp chopped fresh parsley (optional, for garnish)

Instructions:

1. **Prepare the Beef Layer:**
   - Preheat your oven to 375°F (190°C). Heat olive oil in a large skillet over medium heat. Add the ground beef, onion, and garlic. Cook until the beef is browned and the onion is softened, about 5–7 minutes.
   - Stir in the smoked paprika, thyme, cumin, salt, and pepper. Remove from heat and set aside.
2. **Prepare the Sauce:**
   - In a saucepan, heat the cream and milk over medium heat. Whisk in the flour until smooth. Cook for 2–3 minutes, stirring constantly, until the mixture thickens slightly. Season with salt and pepper to taste.
3. **Assemble the Casserole:**
   - Lightly grease a 9x13-inch baking dish. Layer half of the sliced potatoes on the bottom of the dish, overlapping slightly. Spread the beef mixture evenly over the potatoes. Top with the remaining potato slices.
   - Pour the cream sauce over the potatoes, ensuring it seeps into all the layers.
4. **Add the Cheese Topping:**
   - Sprinkle the shredded cheddar and Parmesan cheeses evenly over the top.
5. **Bake to Perfection:**
   - Cover the dish with aluminum foil and bake for 40 minutes. Remove the foil and bake for an additional 20 minutes, or until the potatoes are tender and the cheese is golden and bubbly.
6. **Serve and Enjoy:**
   - Garnish with fresh parsley, if desired, and serve hot. This dish pairs wonderfully with a crisp green salad or roasted vegetables.

The Buried Beef and Potato Bake is a rich, satisfying casserole that brings the depth and warmth of underground flavors to your table.

Digging Deep Shepherd's Pie

Shepherd's pie gets a subterranean twist with this recipe, featuring a root vegetable mash topping that adds earthy sweetness and depth to the traditional dish. Beneath the golden layer lies a savory filling of tender beef and vegetables, simmered in a flavorful gravy.

Ingredients:

For the Filling:

- 1 lb ground lamb or beef
- 1 medium onion, diced
- 2 carrots, diced
- 2 celery stalks, diced
- 1 cup frozen peas
- 2 tbsp tomato paste
- 1 cup beef or vegetable broth
- 2 tsp Worcestershire sauce
- 1 tsp thyme
- 1 tsp rosemary
- Salt and pepper to taste
- 2 tbsp all-purpose flour
- 2 tbsp olive oil

For the Topping:

- 2 large sweet potatoes, peeled and diced
- 2 medium parsnips, peeled and diced
- 1 tbsp butter
- ¼ cup milk
- Salt and pepper to taste

Instructions:

1. **Prepare the Topping:**
   - Boil the sweet potatoes and parsnips in a large pot of salted water until tender, about 15–20 minutes. Drain and mash with the butter, milk, salt, and pepper. Set aside.
2. **Cook the Filling:**
   - Heat olive oil in a large skillet over medium heat. Add the ground meat, onion, carrots, and celery. Cook until the meat is browned and the vegetables are softened, about 8–10 minutes.
   - Stir in the tomato paste, thyme, rosemary, and Worcestershire sauce. Sprinkle the flour over the mixture and stir well. Gradually pour in the broth, stirring constantly, until the filling thickens into a rich gravy. Stir in the peas and season with salt and pepper.
3. **Assemble the Shepherd's Pie:**
   - Preheat your oven to 400°F (200°C). Spread the filling evenly in a 9x9-inch baking dish. Spoon the root vegetable mash over the filling, spreading it evenly with a spatula. Use a fork to create decorative ridges on the surface.
4. **Bake to Perfection:**
   - Bake for 25–30 minutes, or until the topping is golden and slightly crisp. Let cool for 5 minutes before serving.
5. **Serve and Enjoy:**
   - Pair this Digging Deep Shepherd's Pie with a simple side of steamed greens or a crusty bread for a meal that's both comforting and satisfying.

Hearty Underground Casseroles: A Graboid's Feast

Casseroles are the epitome of comfort food, and these recipes deliver layers of bold, satisfying flavors inspired by the Graboids' underground world. The **Buried Beef and Potato Bake** and **Digging Deep Shepherd's Pie** are perfect for cozy family dinners, potlucks, or even as meal-prep options for the week ahead.

These dishes bring the essence of underground cooking to life, combining hearty ingredients, rich gravies, and golden toppings that bubble and brown to perfection. Prepare to dig in—because when it comes to these casseroles, every bite is an adventure worth savoring.

Chapter 8: Fossilized Finger Foods

Finger foods are the life of any gathering, and in this chapter, we're serving up bite-sized creations inspired by the rugged, fossilized landscapes of the Graboids' domain. These dishes are perfect for parties, game nights, or casual evenings when you want something flavorful and easy to eat. **Fossilized Finger Foods** channel the hearty spirit of the underground with bold flavors and satisfying textures that make every bite unforgettable.

The **Crunchy Graboid Chicken Wings** are a spicy, crispy treat that delivers a satisfying crunch, while the **Stone-Baked Mini Calzones** are filled with savory, molten goodness and baked to golden perfection. These recipes are sure to delight your guests and keep the plates empty.

Crunchy Graboid Chicken Wings

These chicken wings are a fiery homage to the Graboid's ferocious nature. Coated in a spiced, crunchy breading and tossed in a smoky, tangy glaze, they're as bold and satisfying as the creatures themselves.

Ingredients:

For the Wings:

- 2 lbs chicken wings, split into flats and drumettes
- 1 cup all-purpose flour
- ½ cup cornstarch
- 1 tsp smoked paprika
- 1 tsp garlic powder
- 1 tsp onion powder
- 1 tsp cayenne pepper
- 1 tsp salt
- ½ tsp black pepper
- Vegetable oil, for frying

For the Sauce:

- ½ cup hot sauce (e.g., Frank's RedHot)
- 2 tbsp butter
- 1 tbsp honey
- 1 tsp Worcestershire sauce
- 1 tsp smoked paprika

Instructions:

1. **Prepare the Wings:**
   - Pat the chicken wings dry with paper towels. In a large bowl, combine the flour, cornstarch, smoked paprika, garlic powder, onion powder, cayenne pepper, salt, and black pepper.
2. **Coat the Wings:**
   - Toss the chicken wings in the flour mixture until well coated. Let them rest for 10 minutes to allow the coating to adhere.
3. **Fry the Wings:**
   - Heat about 2 inches of vegetable oil in a deep skillet or pot to 375°F (190°C). Fry the wings in batches for 8–10 minutes, or until golden brown and crispy. Transfer to a wire rack to drain excess oil.
4. **Make the Sauce:**
   - In a small saucepan, combine the hot sauce, butter, honey, Worcestershire sauce, and smoked paprika. Heat over low heat, stirring, until the butter is melted and the sauce is smooth.
5. **Toss and Serve:**
   - Toss the fried wings in the sauce until evenly coated. Serve hot with celery sticks, carrot sticks, and ranch or blue cheese dressing on the side.

These Crunchy Graboid Chicken Wings are a perfect blend of heat, crunch, and flavor, making them the ultimate crowd-pleaser.

Stone-Baked Mini Calzones

Inspired by the fossilized rock formations of the Graboid's world, these mini calzones are stuffed with gooey cheese and savory fillings, then baked to golden perfection. Perfectly portable, they're an ideal snack or meal on the go.

Ingredients:

For the Dough:

- 2 ¼ tsp active dry yeast
- 1 cup warm water (110°F/45°C)
- 2 ½ cups all-purpose flour
- 1 tsp sugar
- 1 tsp salt
- 2 tbsp olive oil

For the Filling:

- 1 cup ricotta cheese
- 1 cup shredded mozzarella cheese
- ½ cup grated Parmesan cheese
- 1 cup cooked Italian sausage or diced pepperoni (optional)
- ½ cup sautéed mushrooms, diced bell peppers, or spinach
- 1 tsp Italian seasoning
- Salt and pepper to taste

For Assembly:

- 1 egg, beaten (for egg wash)
- ½ cup marinara sauce (for dipping)

Instructions:

1. **Make the Dough:**
   - In a small bowl, dissolve the yeast in warm water with the sugar. Let sit for 5–10 minutes, or until foamy.
   - In a large bowl, combine the flour and salt. Add the yeast mixture and olive oil, mixing until a dough forms. Knead on a floured surface for 8 minutes, or until smooth and elastic. Place the dough in an oiled bowl, cover, and let rise for 1 hour, or until doubled in size.
2. **Prepare the Filling:**
   - In a mixing bowl, combine the ricotta, mozzarella, Parmesan, Italian sausage or pepperoni, vegetables, and Italian seasoning. Season with salt and pepper to taste.
3. **Assemble the Calzones:**
   - Preheat the oven to 425°F (220°C). Divide the dough into 8 equal portions and roll each into a 6-inch circle. Place a heaping spoonful of the filling on one half of each circle, leaving a ½-inch border. Fold the dough over the filling to form a half-moon shape and press the edges to seal. Crimp with a fork for extra security.
4. **Bake to Perfection:**
   - Place the calzones on a parchment-lined baking sheet. Brush the tops with beaten egg for a golden finish. Bake for 15–18 minutes, or until golden brown.
5. **Serve and Enjoy:**
   - Serve the mini calzones warm with marinara sauce for dipping.

These Stone-Baked Mini Calzones are packed with molten goodness in every bite, making them an irresistible addition to your Fossilized Finger Foods lineup.

Fossilized Finger Foods: Bold Bites, Big Flavors

Finger foods are meant to be fun, flavorful, and satisfying, and the **Crunchy Graboid Chicken Wings** and **Stone-Baked Mini Calzones** deliver on all fronts. These dishes are perfect for entertaining or for indulging in a snack that feels like an adventure.

Channeling the spirit of *Tremors*, these recipes bring bold textures and flavors to the table, proving that even the smallest bites can pack the biggest thrills. Get your hands dirty, dig in, and let these fossil-inspired treats become the stars of your next gathering.

Chapter 9: Sand-Sifting Side Dishes

No meal is complete without sides that bring balance, texture, and complementary flavors to the main dishes. In this chapter, we venture into the world of **Sand-Sifting Side Dishes**, inspired by the rugged terrain and resourceful spirit of the Graboids. These sides aren't just after-thoughts—they're bold, satisfying additions that can hold their own at any table.

The **Loaded Twice-Baked Potatoes** are a rich, indulgent take on a classic comfort food, while the **Sandy Spiced Cornbread** combines warm, earthy spices with a tender, crumbly texture. These recipes are perfect for family dinners, potlucks, or simply as a way to elevate your everyday meals.

Loaded Twice-Baked Potatoes

A side dish that feels like a meal in itself, these twice-baked potatoes are loaded with creamy, cheesy filling, savory bacon, and fresh herbs. Their rich, satisfying flavor and crisp edges make them a standout addition to any table.

Ingredients:

- 4 large russet potatoes
- 2 tbsp olive oil
- ½ cup sour cream
- ¼ cup whole milk
- 2 tbsp unsalted butter
- 1 cup shredded cheddar cheese, divided
- ½ cup cooked and crumbled bacon
- 2 green onions, thinly sliced
- Salt and pepper to taste

Instructions:

1. **Bake the Potatoes:**
   - Preheat your oven to 400°F (200°C). Wash the potatoes and pat them dry. Rub each potato with olive oil and prick a few holes in the skin with a fork. Place the potatoes directly on the oven rack and bake for 50–60 minutes, or until tender.
2. **Prepare the Filling:**
   - Let the potatoes cool slightly, then cut each one in half lengthwise. Scoop out the flesh, leaving a ¼-inch border to keep the skin intact. Place the scooped-out potato in a bowl.
   - Mash the potato flesh with the sour cream, milk, butter, and half of the cheddar cheese. Stir in the crumbled bacon and green onions. Season with salt and pepper to taste.
3. **Stuff and Bake Again:**
   - Spoon the filling back into the potato skins, mounding it slightly. Place the stuffed potatoes on a baking sheet. Sprinkle the remaining cheddar cheese over the tops.
   - Return the potatoes to the oven and bake for an additional 15–20 minutes, or until the cheese is melted and golden.

4. **Serve and Enjoy:**
   ◦ Garnish with extra green onions or a dollop of sour cream if desired. Serve hot alongside your favorite main dishes.

These Loaded Twice-Baked Potatoes are indulgent, customizable, and guaranteed to be a hit with any crowd.

Sandy Spiced Cornbread

Cornbread gets a *Tremors* twist in this recipe, featuring a sandy texture that crumbles just enough to make every bite delightful. Spiced with warm, earthy flavors like cumin and smoked paprika, this cornbread is a perfect companion to soups, stews, or grilled dishes.

Ingredients:

- 1 cup yellow cornmeal
- 1 cup all-purpose flour
- 2 tsp baking powder
- ½ tsp baking soda
- 1 tsp salt
- 1 tsp ground cumin
- ½ tsp smoked paprika
- ¼ tsp cayenne pepper (optional, for heat)
- 1 cup buttermilk
- 2 large eggs
- ¼ cup honey
- 4 tbsp unsalted butter, melted and cooled

Instructions:

1. **Preheat the Oven:**
   - Preheat your oven to 375°F (190°C). Grease an 8x8-inch baking pan or cast-iron skillet.
2. **Mix the Dry Ingredients:**
   - In a large bowl, whisk together the cornmeal, flour, baking powder, baking soda, salt, cumin, smoked paprika, and cayenne pepper.
3. **Combine the Wet Ingredients:**
   - In a separate bowl, whisk together the buttermilk, eggs, honey, and melted butter.
4. **Make the Batter:**
   - Pour the wet ingredients into the dry ingredients and stir until just combined. Be careful not to overmix; the batter should be slightly lumpy.
5. **Bake the Cornbread:**
   - Pour the batter into the prepared pan or skillet, spreading it evenly. Bake for 20–25 minutes, or until the top is golden brown and a toothpick inserted in the center comes out clean.
6. **Serve and Enjoy:**
   - Let the cornbread cool slightly before slicing. Serve warm with a drizzle of honey, a pat of butter, or alongside chili, soup, or BBQ dishes.

The Sandy Spiced Cornbread is a deliciously versatile side, with a balance of sweetness and spice that elevates any meal.

Sand-Sifting Side Dishes: Digging Deep into Flavor

Side dishes don't have to play second fiddle—they can steal the show when done right. The **Loaded Twice-Baked Potatoes** and **Sandy Spiced Cornbread** bring bold, comforting flavors that stand out while complementing a variety of main dishes.

These recipes channel the underground essence of the Graboids, combining hearty textures, earthy spices, and a touch of creativity to deliver sides that are unforgettable. Whether you're hosting a dinner party or simply looking to enhance your everyday meals, these sides will leave everyone satisfied and digging in for seconds.

Chapter 10: Creature Comfort Breakfasts

Breakfast is the most important meal of the day, and when inspired by the untamed spirit of the Graboids, it becomes a feast of bold flavors and comforting textures. In this chapter, **Creature Comfort Breakfasts** take center stage with dishes designed to energize your mornings and satisfy your appetite for adventure.

The **Graboid Pancake Stack with Syrupy Lava** delivers towering layers of fluffy pancakes drenched in a molten syrup, while the **Underground Breakfast Casserole** combines hearty ingredients like eggs, sausage, and potatoes into a satisfying, one-dish wonder. Whether you're feeding a family or indulging in a leisurely breakfast, these recipes bring excitement and comfort to the start of your day.

Graboid Pancake Stack with Syrupy Lava

This towering pancake stack is a delicious homage to the Graboids, with layers as thick as the creatures themselves. Topped with a molten "lava" syrup and optional fresh berries, it's a breakfast that's as indulgent as it is impressive.

Ingredients:

For the Pancakes:

- 2 cups all-purpose flour
- 2 tbsp sugar
- 2 tsp baking powder
- ½ tsp baking soda
- ½ tsp salt
- 2 large eggs
- 2 cups buttermilk
- 2 tbsp unsalted butter, melted and cooled
- 1 tsp vanilla extract

For the Syrupy Lava:

- 1 cup maple syrup
- 2 tbsp butter
- 1 tbsp brown sugar
- ½ tsp cinnamon (optional)
- Fresh berries (optional, for garnish)

Instructions:

1. **Prepare the Pancake Batter:**
   - In a large bowl, whisk together the flour, sugar, baking powder, baking soda, and salt. In a separate bowl, whisk together the eggs, buttermilk, melted butter, and vanilla extract. Gradually add the wet ingredients to the dry ingredients, stirring until just combined (a few lumps are fine).
2. **Cook the Pancakes:**
   - Heat a nonstick skillet or griddle over medium heat and lightly grease with butter or cooking spray. Pour ¼ cup of batter onto the skillet for each pancake. Cook until bubbles form on the surface, then flip and cook until golden brown on both sides. Repeat with the remaining batter, stacking the pancakes as you go.
3. **Make the Syrupy Lava:**
   - In a small saucepan, combine the maple syrup, butter, brown sugar, and cinnamon. Heat over low heat, stirring until the butter is melted and the mixture is smooth. Remove from heat and keep warm.
4. **Assemble the Pancake Stack:**
   - Stack the pancakes high on a plate, pouring the syrupy lava generously over the top. Garnish with fresh berries, if desired, for a burst of brightness.
5. **Serve and Enjoy:**
   - Serve immediately with extra syrup on the side for those who dare to dive deeper into sweetness.

The Graboid Pancake Stack with Syrupy Lava is a visually stunning and mouthwatering breakfast that's sure to be a hit with kids and adults alike.

Underground Breakfast Casserole

This hearty breakfast casserole is packed with eggs, sausage, potatoes, and cheese, making it a one-dish meal that's perfect for feeding a crowd. With layers of flavor and texture, it's a dish that brings the warmth and comfort of an underground lair to your breakfast table.

Ingredients:

- 1 lb breakfast sausage (pork, turkey, or vegetarian alternative)
- 1 medium onion, diced
- 1 red bell pepper, diced
- 3 cups frozen hash browns, thawed
- 8 large eggs
- 1 cup whole milk
- 1 cup shredded cheddar cheese
- ½ cup shredded mozzarella cheese
- 1 tsp garlic powder
- 1 tsp smoked paprika
- Salt and pepper to taste
- 2 tbsp chopped fresh parsley (optional, for garnish)

Instructions:

1. **Cook the Sausage and Vegetables:**
   - Preheat your oven to 375°F (190°C). In a large skillet over medium heat, cook the sausage, breaking it into crumbles, until browned and cooked through. Remove the sausage and set aside.
   - In the same skillet, sauté the onion and red bell pepper until softened, about 5 minutes.
2. **Prepare the Casserole Base:**
   - Grease a 9x13-inch baking dish. Spread the thawed hash browns evenly across the bottom. Layer the cooked sausage, onion, and bell pepper on top of the hash browns.
3. **Make the Egg Mixture:**
   - In a large bowl, whisk together the eggs, milk, garlic powder, smoked paprika, salt, and pepper. Pour the egg mixture evenly over the sausage and vegetables in the dish.
4. **Add the Cheese Topping:**
   - Sprinkle the cheddar and mozzarella cheeses evenly over the casserole.
5. **Bake the Casserole:**
   - Cover the dish with aluminum foil and bake for 25 minutes. Remove the foil and bake for an additional 15–20 minutes, or until the eggs are set and the cheese is melted and golden.

6. **Serve and Enjoy:**
   ◦ Let the casserole cool for 5 minutes before garnishing with fresh parsley and slicing into portions. Serve hot with toast or fresh fruit for a complete breakfast.

The Underground Breakfast Casserole is a hearty, crowd-pleasing dish that's perfect for brunches, holidays, or meal prepping for busy mornings.

Creature Comfort Breakfasts: Starting the Day with Bold Flavors

Breakfast is your chance to set the tone for the day, and these recipes deliver a mix of indulgence, creativity, and comfort. The **Graboid Pancake Stack with Syrupy Lava** offers a sweet, towering start to the day, while the **Underground Breakfast Casserole** provides a savory, hearty option that's as practical as it is delicious.

Whether you're preparing a special weekend brunch or looking for a satisfying dish to fuel a busy day, these recipes bring a touch of *Tremors*-inspired adventure to your mornings. Dig in and start your day off right!

Chapter 11: Subterranean Sandwiches

Sandwiches are a cornerstone of quick, satisfying meals, and this chapter takes them to new depths with **Subterranean Sandwiches** inspired by the bold, hearty flavors of the Graboids. These sandwiches are not only packed with layers of delicious ingredients but also designed to evoke the rugged, resourceful spirit of the *Tremors* universe.

The **Tremor Turkey Club** offers a fresh twist on the classic club sandwich with a balance of smoky, savory, and crunchy elements, while **The Graboid Grinder Sub** is a monstrous creation piled high with meats, cheese, and bold seasonings, perfect for anyone with a ferocious appetite. These recipes are versatile, satisfying, and ideal for lunches, picnics, or quick dinners.

Tremor Turkey Club

This turkey club sandwich is a towering masterpiece that combines classic ingredients like turkey, bacon, lettuce, and tomato with bold extras like smoky aioli and toasted bread. Perfectly balanced and satisfying, it's a sandwich that's as unforgettable as a Graboid encounter.

Ingredients:

- 6 slices of sourdough or multigrain bread, toasted
- 8 oz sliced turkey breast (deli or roasted)
- 6 slices of crispy bacon
- 1 large tomato, sliced
- 4 leaves of crisp romaine lettuce
- 2 slices of cheddar or Swiss cheese (optional)
- 3 tbsp mayonnaise
- 1 tsp smoked paprika
- 1 tsp Dijon mustard
- Salt and pepper to taste

Instructions:

1. **Prepare the Smoky Aioli:**
   - In a small bowl, mix the mayonnaise, smoked paprika, and Dijon mustard. Season with salt and pepper to taste.
2. **Toast the Bread:**
   - Lightly toast the bread slices and spread a thin layer of the smoky aioli on one side of each slice.
3. **Assemble the Layers:**
   - Start with one slice of bread as the base. Add a layer of turkey slices, followed by a leaf of lettuce, and a slice of tomato. Season lightly with salt and pepper.

- Place a second slice of bread on top and repeat the layering process with bacon, cheese (if using), another leaf of lettuce, and tomato.
4. **Top It Off:**
   - Finish the sandwich with the final slice of bread, aioli side down. Secure with sandwich picks if needed, and cut diagonally into halves or quarters for easy serving.
5. **Serve and Enjoy:**
   - Pair the Tremor Turkey Club with a side of chips, pickles, or a fresh salad for a complete meal.

This Tremor Turkey Club is the perfect balance of fresh, smoky, and savory flavors, making it a crowd-pleaser for any occasion.

The Graboid Grinder Sub

The Graboid Grinder Sub is a towering, meaty sandwich that channels the ferocity of the Graboids themselves. Packed with deli meats, cheese, vegetables, and a zesty dressing, this sub is as bold and satisfying as it is monstrous.

Ingredients:

- 1 large sub roll or baguette (12 inches), sliced lengthwise
- 4 oz thinly sliced salami
- 4 oz thinly sliced ham
- 4 oz thinly sliced roast beef
- 4 slices of provolone or mozzarella cheese
- 1 cup shredded iceberg lettuce
- ½ cup sliced tomatoes
- ½ cup thinly sliced red onions
- ¼ cup sliced banana peppers (optional)
- 2 tbsp olive oil
- 1 tbsp red wine vinegar
- 1 tsp dried oregano
- 1 tsp garlic powder
- ½ tsp crushed red pepper flakes (optional)
- Salt and pepper to taste

Instructions:

1. **Prepare the Dressing:**
   - In a small bowl, whisk together the olive oil, red wine vinegar, oregano, garlic powder, crushed red pepper flakes, and a pinch of salt and pepper.
2. **Assemble the Sub:**
   - Open the sub roll or baguette and lightly toast it if desired. Layer the bottom half with salami, ham, roast beef, and cheese slices.
3. **Add the Vegetables:**
   - Top the meats with shredded lettuce, sliced tomatoes, red onions, and banana peppers (if using).
4. **Drizzle with Dressing:**
   - Generously drizzle the dressing over the vegetables, allowing it to soak slightly into the bread.
5. **Close and Serve:**
   - Place the top half of the roll on the sandwich, pressing down gently to secure the layers. Slice the sub into portions for easy serving.

6. **Enjoy the Feast:**
   - Pair the Graboid Grinder Sub with chips, a pickle spear, or a side of coleslaw for a hearty meal.

The Graboid Grinder Sub is a flavor-packed, towering creation that's perfect for sharing or tackling solo when you're feeling as hungry as a Graboid.

Subterranean Sandwiches: Layers of Flavor, Depth of Satisfaction

Sandwiches are more than just quick meals—they're an opportunity to experiment with bold flavors and satisfying textures. The **Tremor Turkey Club** and **Graboid Grinder Sub** are towering tributes to this versatile dish, offering layers of hearty ingredients and bold seasonings that deliver big on taste.

Perfect for any time of day, these sandwiches are portable, customizable, and guaranteed to keep you fueled for whatever adventure lies ahead. Whether you're packing a picnic, hosting a casual lunch, or just feeding your inner Graboid, these subterranean sandwiches will not disappoint.

Chapter 12: Carnivore's Delight – Meat Mains

For those who crave the heartiness and bold flavors of expertly prepared meats, **Carnivore's Delight** brings the essence of a Graboid-inspired feast to your table. This chapter is dedicated to indulgent meat-based mains that are as satisfying as they are flavorful.

The **Graboid's Feast Steak with Underground Marinade** delivers a perfectly seared, juicy steak infused with earthy and smoky flavors, while the **Tremor-Stuffed Pork Loin** combines tender pork with a savory stuffing that's rich, flavorful, and perfect for special occasions. These recipes embrace the primal satisfaction of meat-centric dishes, channeling the wild, untamed spirit of *Tremors*.

Graboid's Feast Steak with Underground Marinade

This steak is marinated in a bold, earthy blend of flavors that pays homage to the Graboid's subterranean habitat. The marinade penetrates the meat, enhancing its natural flavor, while the high-heat sear creates a beautiful crust that locks in the juices.

Ingredients:

- 4 ribeye or New York strip steaks (1-inch thick)
- 3 tbsp olive oil
- 3 tbsp soy sauce
- 2 tbsp balsamic vinegar
- 2 cloves garlic, minced
- 1 tsp smoked paprika
- 1 tsp ground cumin
- 1 tsp Dijon mustard
- ½ tsp dried thyme
- ½ tsp black pepper
- ½ tsp salt

Instructions:

1. **Prepare the Marinade:**
   - In a medium bowl, whisk together the olive oil, soy sauce, balsamic vinegar, garlic, smoked paprika, cumin, Dijon mustard, thyme, black pepper, and salt.
2. **Marinate the Steaks:**
   - Place the steaks in a large resealable plastic bag or shallow dish. Pour the marinade over the steaks, ensuring they are evenly coated. Seal the bag or cover the dish and refrigerate for at least 2 hours, or up to 8 hours for deeper flavor.
3. **Preheat the Grill or Pan:**
   - Heat a grill or cast-iron skillet over high heat until very hot. Lightly oil the grates or pan to prevent sticking.

4. **Cook the Steaks:**
   - Remove the steaks from the marinade and pat them dry with paper towels. Cook the steaks for 4–5 minutes per side for medium-rare, or adjust the time to your preferred doneness. Use a meat thermometer to ensure accuracy (125°F/52°C for medium-rare).
5. **Rest and Serve:**
   - Let the steaks rest for 5 minutes before slicing to allow the juices to redistribute. Serve with a side of roasted vegetables, mashed potatoes, or a crisp salad.

The Graboid's Feast Steak with Underground Marinade is a bold and satisfying dish that's perfect for carnivores who appreciate depth of flavor and a perfectly cooked cut of meat.

Tremor-Stuffed Pork Loin

This pork loin is a show-stopping centerpiece, featuring tender meat wrapped around a savory stuffing that combines earthy flavors, herbs, and textures. Perfect for family gatherings or special occasions, this dish is as elegant as it is delicious.

Ingredients:

For the Pork Loin:

- 1 (3-4 lb) pork loin, butterflied and pounded to an even thickness
- 1 tbsp olive oil
- 1 tsp salt
- 1 tsp black pepper
- 1 tsp smoked paprika

For the Stuffing:

- 1 tbsp olive oil
- 1 small onion, finely diced
- 2 cloves garlic, minced
- 1 cup breadcrumbs (panko or traditional)
- ½ cup cooked and crumbled sausage
- ¼ cup chopped dried cranberries or raisins
- ¼ cup chopped fresh parsley
- 1 tsp dried thyme
- 1 tsp sage
- ½ cup chicken broth

Instructions:

1. **Prepare the Stuffing:**
   - Heat olive oil in a skillet over medium heat. Add the onion and garlic, sautéing until softened. Remove from heat and transfer to a bowl.
   - Stir in the breadcrumbs, sausage, cranberries, parsley, thyme, and sage. Gradually add the chicken broth, mixing until the stuffing is moist but not soggy. Set aside to cool.
2. **Prepare the Pork Loin:**
   - Preheat the oven to 375°F (190°C). Lay the butterflied pork loin flat on a clean surface. Spread the stuffing evenly over the pork, leaving a 1-inch border on all sides.
   - Roll the pork tightly into a log, securing it with kitchen twine at 2-inch intervals. Rub the outside with olive oil, salt, pepper, and smoked paprika.
3. **Sear the Pork Loin:**
   - Heat a large oven-safe skillet or roasting pan over medium-high heat. Sear the pork loin on all sides until golden brown, about 2 minutes per side.
4. **Roast the Pork Loin:**
   - Transfer the skillet or roasting pan to the oven. Roast for 45–55 minutes, or until the internal temperature of the pork reaches 145°F (63°C). Baste with pan juices halfway through cooking.
5. **Rest and Serve:**
   - Let the pork loin rest for 10 minutes before slicing. Serve with gravy, roasted vegetables, or a side of mashed sweet potatoes.

The Tremor-Stuffed Pork Loin is a stunning dish that combines tender meat, savory stuffing, and beautiful presentation, making it the perfect choice for a celebratory meal.

Carnivore's Delight: Bold Flavors, Unforgettable Mains

For meat lovers, these recipes are a dream come true. The **Graboid's Feast Steak with Underground Marinade** and **Tremor-Stuffed Pork Loin** offer bold flavors and satisfying textures that elevate any meal to a feast.

Whether you're grilling for a casual dinner or preparing an impressive dish for a special occasion, these meat mains deliver unforgettable flavor and a touch of adventure to your table. Unleash your inner carnivore and dig into the delicious depths of these hearty recipes!

Chapter 13: Vegetarian Vibrations

In the world of *Tremors*, survival means embracing what the land provides, and this chapter proves that vegetarian dishes can be just as hearty, flavorful, and satisfying as their meaty counterparts. **Vegetarian Vibrations** focuses on meals that pack a punch with earthy ingredients, bold seasonings, and satisfying textures that make every bite a celebration of plant-based goodness.

The **Mushroom and Spinach Stuffed Peppers** are colorful, nutrient-packed bundles of flavor, while the **Spaghetti Squash Alfredo with Crispy Sage** transforms simple ingredients into a creamy, indulgent dish with a touch of gourmet flair. These recipes are perfect for vegetarians, flexitarians, or anyone looking to enjoy a lighter, healthier option without sacrificing flavor.

Mushroom and Spinach Stuffed Peppers

Stuffed peppers are a classic vegetarian dish, but this version elevates them with a savory filling of mushrooms, spinach, rice, and cheese. These colorful creations are perfect as a main dish or a hearty side.

Ingredients:

- 4 large bell peppers (any color)
- 1 tbsp olive oil
- 1 medium onion, diced
- 2 cloves garlic, minced
- 2 cups diced mushrooms (cremini, button, or shiitake)
- 2 cups fresh spinach, chopped
- 1 cup cooked rice (white, brown, or wild)
- ½ cup grated Parmesan cheese
- ½ cup shredded mozzarella cheese (optional)
- 1 tsp dried oregano
- ½ tsp smoked paprika
- Salt and pepper to taste
- 1 cup marinara sauce

Instructions:

1. **Prepare the Peppers:**
   - Preheat the oven to 375°F (190°C). Slice the tops off the bell peppers and remove the seeds and membranes. Place the peppers upright in a baking dish.
2. **Cook the Filling:**
   - Heat olive oil in a skillet over medium heat. Add the onion and garlic, sautéing until softened. Add the mushrooms and cook until they release their moisture and begin to brown, about 5–7 minutes.
   - Stir in the spinach and cook until wilted. Remove from heat and mix in the cooked rice, Parmesan cheese, oregano, smoked paprika, salt, and pepper.
3. **Stuff the Peppers:**
   - Spoon the filling into each pepper, packing it tightly. Top with shredded mozzarella cheese, if desired.
4. **Bake the Peppers:**
   - Pour the marinara sauce around the peppers in the baking dish. Cover with foil and bake for 25 minutes. Remove the foil and bake for an additional 10 minutes, or until the peppers are tender and the cheese is golden and bubbly.
5. **Serve and Enjoy:**
   - Plate the peppers with a spoonful of the marinara sauce from the dish. Garnish with fresh herbs, such as parsley or basil, for added brightness.

These Mushroom and Spinach Stuffed Peppers are as beautiful as they are delicious, making them a standout vegetarian main or side dish.

Spaghetti Squash Alfredo with Crispy Sage

Spaghetti squash serves as the perfect base for a rich, creamy Alfredo sauce, while crispy sage leaves add a gourmet touch. This dish is comforting, flavorful, and a fantastic alternative to traditional pasta.

Ingredients:

- 1 large spaghetti squash
- 2 tbsp olive oil, divided
- Salt and pepper to taste
- 3 tbsp unsalted butter
- 2 cloves garlic, minced
- 1 cup heavy cream
- ¾ cup grated Parmesan cheese
- ½ tsp nutmeg (optional)
- 6–8 fresh sage leaves

Instructions:

1. **Roast the Spaghetti Squash:**
   - Preheat the oven to 400°F (200°C). Cut the spaghetti squash in half lengthwise and scoop out the seeds. Drizzle the flesh with 1 tablespoon of olive oil and season with salt and pepper.
   - Place the squash halves cut-side down on a baking sheet and roast for 40–50 minutes, or until the flesh is tender and easily shredded with a fork.
2. **Prepare the Alfredo Sauce:**
   - In a saucepan, melt the butter over medium heat. Add the garlic and sauté until fragrant, about 1 minute. Stir in the heavy cream and bring to a gentle simmer. Slowly whisk in the Parmesan cheese until melted and smooth. Add the nutmeg, if desired, and season with salt and pepper to taste.
3. **Crisp the Sage Leaves:**
   - In a small skillet, heat the remaining tablespoon of olive oil over medium heat. Add the sage leaves and cook for 30 seconds to 1 minute, or until crispy but not browned. Remove and drain on a paper towel.
4. **Assemble the Dish:**
   - Using a fork, scrape the roasted squash flesh into strands and place in a large serving bowl. Pour the Alfredo sauce over the squash and toss gently to combine.
5. **Serve and Garnish:**
   - Divide the squash among plates and top with crispy sage leaves. Serve with extra Parmesan cheese on the side, if desired.

The Spaghetti Squash Alfredo with Crispy Sage is a creamy, satisfying dish that combines comfort and sophistication in every bite.

Vegetarian Vibrations: Bold, Satisfying, and Earthy

These vegetarian recipes prove that meatless dishes can be just as flavorful and satisfying as their carnivorous counterparts. The **Mushroom and Spinach Stuffed Peppers** and **Spaghetti Squash Alfredo with Crispy Sage** showcase the versatility of plant-based ingredients, transforming simple vegetables into gourmet meals.

Perfect for vegetarians and omnivores alike, these dishes bring earthy, bold flavors to the forefront, ensuring that every bite is as enjoyable as it is nourishing. Whether you're cooking for yourself or entertaining guests, these recipes are sure to impress and satisfy.

Chapter 14: Oceanic Echoes – Seafood Specials

The Graboids may be creatures of the land, but this chapter dives deep into the ocean for inspiration. **Oceanic Echoes** features bold, seafood-centric recipes that capture the spirit of adventure and the flavors of the sea. Perfect for lovers of seafood, these dishes bring a fresh, coastal vibe to your table while staying grounded in hearty, satisfying textures.

The **Sand-Crusted Crab Cakes** deliver a crispy, golden crust with a tender, flavorful crab filling, while the **Burrowing Shrimp Scampi** combines succulent shrimp with garlic, butter, and pasta for a dish that's as comforting as it is indulgent. These recipes are versatile enough for casual dinners or special occasions.

Sand-Crusted Crab Cakes

These crab cakes are coated in a crispy breadcrumb mixture that gives them a "sand-crusted" texture, while the interior remains tender and bursting with flavor. Serve them as a main dish, appetizer, or even in a sandwich for a versatile seafood treat.

Ingredients:

For the Crab Cakes:

- 1 lb lump crab meat (picked over for shells)
- ½ cup panko breadcrumbs
- ¼ cup mayonnaise
- 1 egg, beaten
- 1 tsp Dijon mustard
- 1 tsp Old Bay seasoning
- 1 tsp Worcestershire sauce
- 1 tbsp chopped fresh parsley
- 1 tbsp lemon juice
- ½ tsp garlic powder
- Salt and pepper to taste

For the Crust and Cooking:

- ½ cup panko breadcrumbs
- ½ cup crushed saltine crackers or breadcrumbs
- 2 tbsp olive oil or butter for frying

For the Sauce (optional):

- ½ cup mayonnaise
- 1 tbsp lemon juice

- 1 tsp Dijon mustard
- 1 tsp Old Bay seasoning

Instructions:

1. **Prepare the Crab Cake Mixture:**
   - In a large bowl, gently combine the crab meat, breadcrumbs, mayonnaise, egg, Dijon mustard, Old Bay seasoning, Worcestershire sauce, parsley, lemon juice, garlic powder, salt, and pepper. Be careful not to break up the crab meat too much.
2. **Form the Crab Cakes:**
   - Shape the mixture into 8 patties, about ½ inch thick. Place the patties on a baking sheet and refrigerate for at least 30 minutes to help them firm up.
3. **Prepare the Crust:**
   - In a shallow dish, mix the panko breadcrumbs and crushed saltine crackers. Lightly press each crab cake into the mixture, coating both sides.
4. **Cook the Crab Cakes:**
   - Heat olive oil or butter in a large skillet over medium heat. Fry the crab cakes in batches for 3–4 minutes per side, or until golden brown and crispy. Transfer to a paper towel-lined plate to drain excess oil.
5. **Prepare the Sauce (Optional):**
   - In a small bowl, mix the mayonnaise, lemon juice, Dijon mustard, and Old Bay seasoning. Serve alongside the crab cakes for dipping.
6. **Serve and Enjoy:**
   - Plate the crab cakes with a side of coleslaw, lemon wedges, or a simple salad for a complete meal.

These Sand-Crusted Crab Cakes are crispy, flavorful, and guaranteed to bring a taste of the sea to your table.

Burrowing Shrimp Scampi

This shrimp scampi is a luxurious dish that pairs tender shrimp with a rich, buttery garlic sauce and pasta. The flavors of white wine, lemon, and herbs bring brightness and depth to the dish, making it a perfect choice for a quick yet elegant dinner.

Ingredients:

- 1 lb large shrimp, peeled and deveined
- 12 oz linguine or spaghetti
- 3 tbsp unsalted butter
- 2 tbsp olive oil
- 4 cloves garlic, minced
- ½ cup dry white wine (or chicken broth)
- ½ cup seafood or chicken broth
- 1 tbsp lemon juice (plus lemon wedges for serving)
- 1 tsp red pepper flakes (optional)
- ¼ cup chopped fresh parsley
- Salt and pepper to taste

Instructions:

1. **Cook the Pasta:**
   - Bring a large pot of salted water to a boil. Cook the pasta according to package instructions until al dente. Reserve ½ cup of pasta water, then drain the pasta and set aside.
2. **Cook the Shrimp:**
   - Heat 1 tablespoon of butter and 1 tablespoon of olive oil in a large skillet over medium-high heat. Season the shrimp with salt and pepper, then cook for 2–3 minutes per side, or until pink and opaque. Remove the shrimp from the skillet and set aside.
3. **Make the Sauce:**
   - In the same skillet, add the remaining butter and olive oil. Add the garlic and red pepper flakes (if using) and sauté for 1 minute, or until fragrant. Stir in the white wine and broth, scraping up any browned bits from the bottom of the pan. Simmer for 3–4 minutes, or until the liquid is slightly reduced.
4. **Combine and Toss:**
   - Add the cooked shrimp back to the skillet along with the cooked pasta. Toss everything together to coat the pasta in the sauce. If the sauce is too thick, add a splash of the reserved pasta water. Stir in the lemon juice and parsley.
5. **Serve and Enjoy:**
   - Divide the scampi among plates and garnish with extra parsley and lemon wedges. Serve with crusty bread for soaking up the sauce.

The Burrowing Shrimp Scampi is a delightful combination of rich, buttery flavors and bright citrus notes, making it a dish that's as elegant as it is comforting.

Oceanic Echoes: Bold Flavors from the Depths

Seafood dishes have a way of bringing a sense of adventure to the table, and these recipes are no exception. The **Sand-Crusted Crab Cakes** and **Burrowing Shrimp Scampi** celebrate the best of oceanic flavors with bold seasonings, satisfying textures, and versatile options for casual or formal dining.

Whether you're hosting a dinner party or treating yourself to a gourmet experience at home, these seafood specials are guaranteed to make a splash. Dive in and let the flavors transport you to the depths of culinary delight.

Chapter 15: Global Graboid Flavors

The *Tremors* universe spans deserts and rugged terrains, but the inspiration for this chapter extends to flavors from around the globe. **Global Graboid Flavors** celebrates the rich culinary traditions of Morocco and Thailand, bringing bold spices and layered aromas to the table. These recipes embody the adventurous spirit of the Graboids, blending cultural authenticity with a touch of creativity.

The **Desert Spice Moroccan Tagine** captures the earthy warmth of North African spices, while the **Spicy Thai Underground Curry** delivers a fiery, flavorful experience inspired by Thailand's vibrant cuisine. These dishes are perfect for those who love bold, aromatic meals that transport their taste buds to distant lands.

Desert Spice Moroccan Tagine

This Moroccan-inspired tagine is a hearty, aromatic stew featuring tender vegetables, dried fruits, and a rich blend of spices. Traditionally cooked in a tagine pot, this recipe can also be prepared in a Dutch oven or heavy-bottomed pot. Serve with fluffy couscous to soak up the flavorful sauce.

Ingredients:

- 2 tbsp olive oil
- 1 large onion, diced
- 3 cloves garlic, minced
- 1 medium sweet potato, peeled and diced
- 1 medium zucchini, diced
- 1 cup chickpeas (canned or cooked)
- ½ cup dried apricots, chopped
- ½ cup golden raisins or sultanas
- 1 (14 oz) can diced tomatoes
- 1 cup vegetable broth
- 1 tsp ground cinnamon
- 1 tsp ground cumin
- 1 tsp ground coriander
- 1 tsp turmeric
- ½ tsp smoked paprika
- ½ tsp cayenne pepper (optional, for heat)
- Salt and pepper to taste
- ¼ cup chopped fresh cilantro (for garnish)
- Toasted slivered almonds (optional, for garnish)

Instructions:

1. **Sauté the Aromatics:**
   - Heat olive oil in a tagine, Dutch oven, or heavy-bottomed pot over medium heat. Add the onion and garlic, sautéing until softened and fragrant, about 5 minutes.
2. **Build the Base:**
   - Stir in the cinnamon, cumin, coriander, turmeric, smoked paprika, and cayenne pepper. Cook for 1–2 minutes, allowing the spices to bloom.
3. **Add the Vegetables:**
   - Add the sweet potato, zucchini, chickpeas, dried apricots, and raisins. Stir to coat the vegetables in the spices.
4. **Simmer the Tagine:**
   - Pour in the diced tomatoes and vegetable broth. Bring the mixture to a simmer, then reduce the heat to low, cover, and cook for 25–30 minutes, or until the vegetables are tender and the flavors have melded.
5. **Serve and Garnish:**
   - Taste and adjust seasoning with salt and pepper. Serve the tagine over couscous or rice, garnished with fresh cilantro and toasted slivered almonds for added texture.

The Desert Spice Moroccan Tagine is a hearty, flavorful dish that combines sweet, savory, and spicy elements for a meal that feels like a warm embrace.

Spicy Thai Underground Curry

This Thai-inspired curry brings bold, fiery flavors to the forefront with a rich coconut milk base, vibrant vegetables, and tender protein. Customize the level of spice to suit your taste, and serve with jasmine rice for a complete meal.

Ingredients:

- 2 tbsp vegetable oil
- 3 tbsp red curry paste
- 1 (13.5 oz) can coconut milk
- 1 cup chicken or vegetable broth
- 1 tbsp fish sauce (or soy sauce for vegetarian option)
- 1 tsp sugar
- 1 lb protein of choice (chicken, shrimp, tofu, or mixed vegetables)
- 1 cup diced carrots
- 1 cup broccoli florets
- 1 red bell pepper, sliced
- ½ cup bamboo shoots (optional)
- 1 tbsp lime juice
- ¼ cup chopped fresh basil or cilantro (for garnish)
- Sliced red chili (optional, for garnish)

Instructions:

1. **Cook the Curry Paste:**
   - Heat the vegetable oil in a large skillet or wok over medium heat. Add the red curry paste and sauté for 1–2 minutes, stirring constantly, until fragrant.
2. **Build the Curry Base:**
   - Stir in the coconut milk, chicken or vegetable broth, fish sauce, and sugar. Bring the mixture to a simmer.
3. **Add the Protein and Vegetables:**
   - Add your protein of choice and cook until tender (e.g., chicken for 10–12 minutes, shrimp for 4–5 minutes, or tofu for 5–7 minutes). Add the carrots, broccoli, bell pepper, and bamboo shoots, simmering until the vegetables are tender but still vibrant, about 5–7 minutes.
4. **Finish the Curry:**
   - Stir in the lime juice and taste, adjusting seasoning with additional fish sauce or sugar as needed.

5. **Serve and Garnish:**
    ◦ Serve the curry over jasmine rice, garnished with fresh basil or cilantro and sliced red chili for an extra kick of heat.

The Spicy Thai Underground Curry is a vibrant, flavorful dish that combines the richness of coconut milk with the heat of Thai spices for a truly unforgettable meal.

Global Graboid Flavors: A Culinary Journey

These globally inspired recipes are a testament to the power of bold spices and rich culinary traditions. The **Desert Spice Moroccan Tagine** and **Spicy Thai Underground Curry** bring the flavors of Morocco and Thailand to life, offering dishes that are hearty, aromatic, and deeply satisfying.

Perfect for adventurous eaters or those looking to expand their culinary horizons, these recipes are as vibrant and diverse as the landscapes that inspired them. Dive into the flavors of the world and let these dishes transport you to distant culinary realms.

Chapter 16: Eruptive Entrees

This chapter brings the excitement of *Tremors*-inspired dishes to life with **Eruptive Entrees**, recipes designed to explode with bold flavors and dynamic presentations. These dishes are hearty, satisfying, and brimming with the kind of layered complexity that mirrors the fiery, unpredictable world of the Graboids.

The **Lava Flow Lasagna** is a rich, indulgent casserole with layers of cheesy, saucy goodness, while the **Volcano Beef Stir-Fry** offers a fiery, vibrant medley of beef, vegetables, and a spicy sauce that's sure to ignite your taste buds. Whether for a family gathering or a thrilling dinner night, these recipes bring drama and deliciousness to your table.

Lava Flow Lasagna

This lasagna is a molten masterpiece of flavors, with layers of pasta, a robust meat sauce, creamy ricotta, and gooey melted cheese. The vibrant red marinara sauce evokes the image of flowing lava, making this dish both visually stunning and deeply satisfying.

Ingredients:

For the Meat Sauce:

- 2 tbsp olive oil
- 1 medium onion, finely diced
- 3 cloves garlic, minced
- 1 lb ground beef or Italian sausage
- 1 (28 oz) can crushed tomatoes
- 2 tbsp tomato paste
- 1 tsp sugar
- 1 tsp dried basil
- 1 tsp dried oregano
- ½ tsp red pepper flakes (optional, for heat)
- Salt and pepper to taste

For the Cheese Mixture:

- 2 cups ricotta cheese
- 1 large egg
- ¼ cup grated Parmesan cheese
- 2 tbsp chopped fresh parsley
- Salt and pepper to taste

For Assembly:

- 12 lasagna noodles, cooked according to package instructions
- 3 cups shredded mozzarella cheese

- ½ cup grated Parmesan cheese

Instructions:

1. **Prepare the Meat Sauce:**
   - Heat olive oil in a large skillet or saucepan over medium heat. Add the onion and garlic, sautéing until softened. Add the ground beef or sausage and cook until browned, breaking it into crumbles as it cooks. Drain excess fat if necessary.
   - Stir in the crushed tomatoes, tomato paste, sugar, basil, oregano, red pepper flakes, salt, and pepper. Simmer for 20 minutes, stirring occasionally, until the sauce thickens.
2. **Prepare the Cheese Mixture:**
   - In a medium bowl, combine the ricotta cheese, egg, Parmesan cheese, parsley, salt, and pepper. Mix well and set aside.
3. **Assemble the Lasagna:**
   - Preheat your oven to 375°F (190°C). Lightly grease a 9x13-inch baking dish. Spread a thin layer of meat sauce on the bottom of the dish.
   - Layer 3 lasagna noodles over the sauce, then spread ⅓ of the ricotta mixture over the noodles. Sprinkle 1 cup of mozzarella cheese on top, followed by ⅓ of the meat sauce. Repeat the layers two more times, finishing with a layer of meat sauce and the remaining mozzarella and Parmesan cheese.
4. **Bake the Lasagna:**
   - Cover the dish with foil and bake for 25 minutes. Remove the foil and bake for an additional 15 minutes, or until the cheese is melted and bubbly.
5. **Serve and Enjoy:**
   - Let the lasagna rest for 10 minutes before slicing and serving. Pair with garlic bread and a crisp green salad for a complete meal.

The Lava Flow Lasagna is a decadent, comforting dish that's sure to become a family favorite.

Volcano Beef Stir-Fry

This stir-fry is a fiery explosion of flavor, featuring tender beef, vibrant vegetables, and a spicy sauce that brings the heat. Quick to prepare and endlessly customizable, it's perfect for busy weeknights or when you crave a dish with bold, eruptive energy.

Ingredients:

For the Stir-Fry Sauce:

- 3 tbsp soy sauce
- 2 tbsp oyster sauce
- 1 tbsp hoisin sauce
- 1 tbsp rice vinegar
- 1 tbsp chili garlic sauce or sriracha
- 1 tsp sesame oil
- 1 tsp cornstarch

For the Stir-Fry:

- 1 lb beef sirloin or flank steak, thinly sliced
- 2 tbsp vegetable oil, divided
- 1 red bell pepper, thinly sliced
- 1 yellow bell pepper, thinly sliced
- 1 cup broccoli florets
- 1 medium carrot, julienned
- 2 green onions, chopped
- 2 cloves garlic, minced
- 1 tsp grated fresh ginger

Instructions:

1. **Prepare the Sauce:**
   - In a small bowl, whisk together the soy sauce, oyster sauce, hoisin sauce, rice vinegar, chili garlic sauce, sesame oil, and cornstarch. Set aside.
2. **Cook the Beef:**
   - Heat 1 tablespoon of vegetable oil in a large skillet or wok over high heat. Add the sliced beef and cook for 2–3 minutes, stirring frequently, until browned but not overcooked. Remove the beef from the skillet and set aside.
3. **Cook the Vegetables:**
   - Add the remaining tablespoon of vegetable oil to the skillet. Stir in the bell peppers, broccoli, carrot, green onions, garlic, and ginger. Cook for 3–5 minutes, stirring often, until the vegetables are tender-crisp.
4. **Combine and Sauce:**
   - Return the beef to the skillet with the vegetables. Pour the sauce over the mixture and stir well to coat. Cook for an additional 2–3 minutes, or until the sauce thickens and evenly coats the beef and vegetables.
5. **Serve and Enjoy:**
   - Serve the stir-fry over steamed jasmine rice or noodles. Garnish with additional green onions or sesame seeds for extra flavor and texture.

The Volcano Beef Stir-Fry is a vibrant, flavorful dish that's as exciting to prepare as it is to eat.

Eruptive Entrees: Bursting with Boldness

These recipes bring excitement to the table, combining rich, layered flavors with dramatic presentation. The **Lava Flow Lasagna** offers a comforting, indulgent experience, while the **Volcano Beef Stir-Fry** delivers a fiery burst of flavor in every bite.

Perfect for family dinners, gatherings, or simply satisfying your craving for something bold and hearty, these **Eruptive Entrees** ensure that your meal is always an adventure. Prepare for an explosion of taste and dig in!

Chapter 17: Campfire Comforts

There's something magical about cooking over a fire, where the rustic charm of the outdoors meets the rich, smoky flavors of campfire cuisine. **Campfire Comforts** brings this magic to life with dishes inspired by the rugged survivalist spirit of *Tremors*. These recipes are perfect for outdoor enthusiasts or anyone who wants to recreate the cozy, nostalgic feel of a campfire meal.

The **Tremor Tin Foil Dinners** are customizable, all-in-one meals cooked directly over hot coals, while the **Smoky Campfire Chili** is a hearty, slow-cooked dish that warms the soul. Easy to prepare and packed with flavor, these recipes are ideal for camping trips or backyard adventures.

Tremor Tin Foil Dinners

Tin foil dinners are the ultimate campfire meal—simple, versatile, and packed with flavor. These customizable packets of meat, vegetables, and seasonings cook to perfection in hot coals, making them a hearty and satisfying choice for outdoor dining.

Ingredients (per packet):

- ½ lb ground beef, chicken, or sausage (or plant-based alternative)
- 1 small potato, diced
- ½ cup diced carrots
- ½ cup diced zucchini or bell peppers
- 2 tbsp butter or olive oil
- 1 tsp garlic powder
- 1 tsp smoked paprika
- Salt and pepper to taste
- Optional toppings: shredded cheese, sour cream, or hot sauce

Instructions:

1. **Prepare the Foil Packets:**
   - Tear off a large sheet of heavy-duty aluminum foil (about 12x18 inches). If using regular foil, double-layer it for durability. Lightly grease the center with butter or olive oil.
2. **Assemble the Ingredients:**
   - Place the ground meat in the center of the foil. Top with the diced potatoes, carrots, zucchini, or bell peppers. Add butter or drizzle with olive oil, then sprinkle with garlic powder, smoked paprika, salt, and pepper.
3. **Seal the Packets:**
   - Fold the sides of the foil up and over the ingredients, then crimp the edges tightly to seal the packet. Make sure there are no gaps where juices can escape.

4. **Cook the Packets:**
    - Place the foil packets directly on hot campfire coals or a grill over medium heat. Cook for 20–25 minutes, flipping halfway through, until the meat is cooked through and the vegetables are tender.
5. **Serve and Enjoy:**
    - Carefully open the packets (beware of steam) and serve directly in the foil for an easy, mess-free meal. Add optional toppings like shredded cheese or sour cream for extra flavor.

The Tremor Tin Foil Dinners are hearty, customizable, and perfect for outdoor adventures.

Smoky Campfire Chili

This smoky, rich chili is the epitome of campfire comfort food. Slow-cooked in a Dutch oven or large pot over a fire, it combines bold spices, tender meat, and beans for a meal that's as warming as the flames themselves.

Ingredients:

- 2 tbsp vegetable oil
- 1 large onion, diced
- 3 cloves garlic, minced
- 1 lb ground beef or turkey (or plant-based ground meat)
- 1 (15 oz) can kidney beans, drained and rinsed
- 1 (15 oz) can black beans, drained and rinsed
- 1 (28 oz) can diced tomatoes
- 1 cup tomato sauce
- 1 cup beef or vegetable broth
- 1 tbsp chili powder
- 1 tsp cumin
- 1 tsp smoked paprika
- ½ tsp cayenne pepper (optional, for heat)
- 1 tsp salt
- ½ tsp black pepper
- Optional toppings: shredded cheese, sour cream, chopped green onions, or tortilla chips

Instructions:

1. **Sauté the Aromatics:**
   - Heat vegetable oil in a Dutch oven or large pot over the campfire. Add the onion and garlic, sautéing until softened and fragrant, about 5 minutes.
2. **Cook the Meat:**
   - Add the ground meat and cook, breaking it into crumbles, until browned and cooked through. Drain any excess fat if necessary.
3. **Add the Beans and Tomatoes:**
   - Stir in the kidney beans, black beans, diced tomatoes, and tomato sauce. Mix well to combine.
4. **Season and Simmer:**
   - Add the beef or vegetable broth, chili powder, cumin, smoked paprika, cayenne pepper, salt, and black pepper. Stir to distribute the spices evenly. Cover the pot with a lid and simmer over low heat for 30–45 minutes, stirring occasionally. Add more broth if the chili becomes too thick.

5. **Serve and Garnish:**
   - Ladle the chili into bowls and top with shredded cheese, sour cream, chopped green onions, or crushed tortilla chips as desired. Serve with cornbread or crusty bread for a complete meal.

The Smoky Campfire Chili is a comforting, flavorful dish that's perfect for chilly nights around the fire.

Campfire Comforts: Rustic and Satisfying

Cooking over a fire brings a sense of adventure and nostalgia to any meal, and these recipes capture that magic perfectly. The **Tremor Tin Foil Dinners** are versatile, easy-to-make packets of flavor, while the **Smoky Campfire Chili** delivers bold, warming comfort with every spoonful.

Whether you're out in the wilderness or enjoying a backyard fire pit, these **Campfire Comforts** bring the cozy charm and hearty flavors of campfire cooking to your table. Dig in and savor the taste of adventure!

Chapter 18: Sweet Tremors – Desserts

After indulging in the bold, savory dishes inspired by the Graboids, it's time to satisfy your sweet tooth with **Sweet Tremors – Desserts**. These creations bring a dramatic flair to the end of your meal, combining irresistible flavors with eye-catching presentations that echo the themes of *Tremors*.

The **Chocolate Lava Cakes** are molten masterpieces with rich, gooey centers that erupt with flavor, while the **Rock Candy Crunch Bars** deliver a delightful mix of textures and sweetness, inspired by the jagged terrain of the Graboids' underground world. These desserts are sure to impress and delight any crowd, making them the perfect finale to your *Tremors*-themed feast.

Chocolate Lava Cakes

Chocolate lava cakes are the ultimate indulgence, with a rich, decadent exterior and a molten, flowing chocolate center. These individual cakes are surprisingly simple to make yet deliver a show-stopping dessert experience.

Ingredients (makes 4 cakes):

- 4 oz semisweet or bittersweet chocolate, chopped
- ½ cup unsalted butter (1 stick)
- 2 large eggs
- 2 large egg yolks
- ¼ cup granulated sugar
- 2 tbsp all-purpose flour
- ¼ tsp salt
- Optional toppings: powdered sugar, whipped cream, or vanilla ice cream

Instructions:

1. **Preheat and Prepare Ramekins:**
   - Preheat your oven to 425°F (220°C). Grease four 6-ounce ramekins with butter and lightly dust with flour, tapping out the excess. Place the ramekins on a baking sheet.
2. **Melt the Chocolate and Butter:**
   - In a heatproof bowl set over a pot of simmering water (or using a microwave in 30-second intervals), melt the chocolate and butter together, stirring until smooth. Remove from heat and let cool slightly.
3. **Mix the Batter:**
   - In a separate bowl, whisk the eggs, egg yolks, and sugar until light and fluffy, about 1–2 minutes. Gently fold in the melted chocolate mixture. Sift the flour and salt over the batter and fold until just combined.

4. **Fill the Ramekins:**
    - Divide the batter evenly among the prepared ramekins, filling each about three-quarters full.
5. **Bake the Cakes:**
    - Bake for 12–14 minutes, or until the edges are set but the centers are still soft and slightly jiggly. Do not overbake, as the molten center is the key feature.
6. **Serve Immediately:**
    - Let the cakes cool for 1 minute, then carefully run a knife around the edges and invert each ramekin onto a plate. Dust with powdered sugar or serve with a scoop of vanilla ice cream for an added indulgence.

The Chocolate Lava Cakes are a dramatic and delicious dessert that's sure to leave your guests in awe.

Rock Candy Crunch Bars

Inspired by the jagged, rocky terrain of the Graboids' underground world, these no-bake Rock Candy Crunch Bars are a textural delight. Sweet, crunchy, and easy to make, they're perfect for snacking or as a sweet treat to end any meal.

Ingredients:

- 2 cups rice cereal (e.g., Rice Krispies)
- 1 cup crushed pretzels
- 1 cup chopped nuts (e.g., almonds, pecans, or peanuts)
- 1 cup mini marshmallows
- 1 cup semisweet chocolate chips
- 1 cup butterscotch chips
- ½ cup creamy peanut butter
- ¼ cup honey or light corn syrup

Instructions:

1. **Prepare the Pan:**
   - Line an 8x8-inch baking pan with parchment paper, leaving an overhang for easy removal.
2. **Combine the Dry Ingredients:**
   - In a large mixing bowl, combine the rice cereal, crushed pretzels, chopped nuts, and mini marshmallows. Stir to evenly distribute the ingredients.
3. **Melt the Chocolate Mixture:**
   - In a heatproof bowl set over a pot of simmering water (or using a microwave in 30-second intervals), melt the chocolate chips, butterscotch chips, peanut butter, and honey. Stir until smooth and well combined.
4. **Mix and Press:**
   - Pour the melted chocolate mixture over the dry ingredients and stir until everything is evenly coated. Transfer the mixture to the prepared pan and press firmly into an even layer using a spatula or the back of a spoon.
5. **Chill and Set:**
   - Refrigerate the bars for at least 1 hour, or until firm.
6. **Slice and Serve:**
   - Lift the bars out of the pan using the parchment paper overhang and cut into squares or rectangles. Serve as is or package them for an on-the-go treat.

The Rock Candy Crunch Bars are a delightful mix of sweet and salty, with a satisfying crunch that makes them irresistible.

Sweet Tremors: A Grand Finale

Desserts are the perfect way to end any meal, and **Sweet Tremors – Desserts** delivers dramatic, indulgent options that are as visually impressive as they are delicious. The **Chocolate Lava Cakes** bring molten decadence to the table, while the **Rock Candy Crunch Bars** offer a fun, textural treat inspired by the Graboids' rocky underground world.

Whether you're hosting a dinner party, celebrating a special occasion, or just treating yourself, these recipes ensure your meal ends on a high note. Dig into these sweet creations and let the flavors and textures take you on a delicious adventure.

Chapter 19: Beverages to Quench the Beast

No feast inspired by *Tremors* is complete without beverages to match the boldness of the menu. In **Beverages to Quench the Beast**, we delve into drinks that bring a playful, thematic twist to classic refreshments. Whether you're hosting a movie night, a themed dinner party, or simply looking for unique drink ideas, these recipes will help you quench your thirst and your imagination.

The **Underground Root Beer Floats** are a nostalgic, family-friendly treat with a nod to the Graboids' subterranean world, while the **Tremor's Sandstorm Cocktails** evoke the dusty chaos of Perfection Valley in a vibrant and boozy concoction. These beverages are designed to delight both kids and adults, offering something special for everyone at the table.

Underground Root Beer Floats

A classic root beer float gets a fun, underground twist with layers of frothy root beer and creamy vanilla ice cream, topped with edible "dirt" for a playful homage to the Graboids' underground habitat.

Ingredients (per serving):

- 1 scoop vanilla ice cream
- 1 cup root beer (chilled)
- 2 tbsp crushed chocolate cookies (e.g., Oreos, for "dirt")
- Optional toppings: whipped cream, chocolate syrup, maraschino cherries

Instructions:

1. **Prepare the Glass:**
    - Select a tall glass or mason jar. For extra flair, dip the rim in chocolate syrup and coat with crushed chocolate cookies.
2. **Layer the Float:**
    - Add a scoop of vanilla ice cream to the glass. Slowly pour the root beer over the ice cream, allowing it to froth and bubble.
3. **Add the Edible Dirt:**
    - Sprinkle the crushed chocolate cookies on top of the float to create an "underground" effect.
4. **Optional Garnishes:**
    - Top with whipped cream, a drizzle of chocolate syrup, or a maraschino cherry for added indulgence.
5. **Serve and Enjoy:**
    - Serve immediately with a straw and spoon. Watch the frothy layers mimic the activity of an underground Graboid!

The Underground Root Beer Floats are a fun, interactive drink that's perfect for kids and adults alike, bringing sweet nostalgia and creativity to the table.

Tremor's Sandstorm Cocktails

This bold and vibrant cocktail captures the essence of a *Tremors*-style sandstorm, blending layers of citrus, spice, and a hint of heat. With its swirling colors and fiery kick, this drink is as exciting to look at as it is to sip.

Ingredients (per cocktail):

- 1 ½ oz tequila
- ½ oz triple sec
- 2 oz orange juice
- 1 oz pineapple juice
- ½ oz grenadine
- ½ tsp chili powder (optional, for rim)
- 1 tsp sugar (optional, for rim)
- Ice
- Optional garnishes: orange slice, maraschino cherry

Instructions:

1. **Prepare the Glass:**
    - Combine the chili powder and sugar on a small plate. Moisten the rim of a cocktail glass with a slice of orange and dip it into the chili-sugar mixture to coat.
2. **Mix the Cocktail:**
    - Fill a cocktail shaker with ice. Add the tequila, triple sec, orange juice, and pineapple juice. Shake vigorously until well chilled.
3. **Create the Sandstorm Effect:**
    - Strain the cocktail into the prepared glass filled with ice. Slowly pour the grenadine down the side of the glass; it will sink to the bottom and gradually rise, creating a swirling "sandstorm" effect.
4. **Garnish and Serve:**
    - Garnish with an orange slice and a maraschino cherry for a pop of color.
5. **Enjoy the Storm:**
    - Serve immediately and let your guests marvel at the dynamic layers before sipping.

The Tremor's Sandstorm Cocktails are a striking and flavorful drink that's perfect for adult gatherings, adding a touch of drama and excitement to any event.

Beverages to Quench the Beast: Fun and Flavorful

Drinks are an essential part of any meal, and **Beverages to Quench the Beast** offers playful and bold options that complement the *Tremors*-inspired menu perfectly. The **Underground Root Beer Floats** bring a sweet, nostalgic charm, while the **Tremor's Sandstorm Cocktails** add a fiery flair that's sure to impress.

Whether you're catering to kids or adults, these beverages are guaranteed to enhance your event and leave everyone talking. Raise your glasses to the Graboids and enjoy these creative, delicious drinks!

Chapter 20: Festive Graboid Feasts

When the holidays roll around, there's nothing quite like gathering loved ones for a grand feast filled with warmth, laughter, and delicious food. **Festive Graboid Feasts** takes inspiration from the subterranean world of the Graboids and infuses it with the joy of holiday traditions, creating centerpiece dishes that are both impressive and full of flavor.

The **Holiday Underground Ham** is a sweet and savory glazed ham with earthy notes, perfect for any festive occasion. The **Sand-Seared Turkey with All the Fixings** transforms a classic roast turkey into a flavorful masterpiece accompanied by comforting sides. These dishes are designed to bring the bold spirit of *Tremors* to your holiday table, ensuring a memorable celebration for all.

Holiday Underground Ham

A glazed ham is a holiday classic, but this version adds a subterranean twist with earthy spices and a rich, sweet glaze. The combination of honey, brown sugar, and mustard creates a beautifully caramelized crust that pairs perfectly with the tender, salty ham.

Ingredients:

- 1 (8–10 lb) bone-in spiral-cut ham
- 1 cup honey
- ¾ cup brown sugar
- 2 tbsp Dijon mustard
- 1 tbsp apple cider vinegar
- 1 tsp ground cinnamon
- ½ tsp ground cloves
- ¼ tsp cayenne pepper (optional, for a hint of heat)

Instructions:

1. **Prepare the Ham:**
   - Preheat your oven to 325°F (165°C). Place the ham cut-side down in a roasting pan and cover loosely with aluminum foil.
2. **Make the Glaze:**
   - In a small saucepan over medium heat, combine the honey, brown sugar, Dijon mustard, apple cider vinegar, cinnamon, cloves, and cayenne pepper. Stir until the sugar is dissolved and the mixture is smooth. Simmer for 2–3 minutes, then remove from heat.
3. **Bake the Ham:**
   - Bake the ham for 1½ hours, basting every 30 minutes with the glaze. Remove the foil during the last 30 minutes of cooking to allow the glaze to caramelize.
4. **Serve and Enjoy:**
   - Let the ham rest for 10 minutes before slicing. Serve with sides like mashed potatoes, roasted vegetables, or cranberry sauce for a complete holiday feast.

The Holiday Underground Ham is a stunning centerpiece with a perfect balance of sweet, savory, and spiced flavors, making it a guaranteed hit for your festive table.

Sand-Seared Turkey with All the Fixings

This roast turkey is seared and seasoned with a bold blend of spices before being roasted to golden perfection. Paired with classic holiday sides like stuffing, gravy, and cranberry sauce, it's a show-stopping dish that captures the essence of a festive feast.

Ingredients:

For the Turkey:

- 1 (12–14 lb) whole turkey, thawed and giblets removed
- ½ cup unsalted butter, softened
- 2 tbsp olive oil
- 1 tbsp smoked paprika
- 1 tbsp garlic powder
- 1 tbsp onion powder
- 2 tsp dried thyme
- 2 tsp ground cumin
- 1 tsp ground sage
- Salt and pepper to taste
- 1 lemon, quartered
- 1 onion, quartered
- 4 sprigs fresh rosemary

For the Gravy:

- 2 tbsp unsalted butter
- 2 tbsp all-purpose flour
- 2 cups turkey drippings or chicken broth
- Salt and pepper to taste

Instructions:

1. **Prepare the Turkey:**
   - Preheat your oven to 325°F (165°C). Pat the turkey dry with paper towels. Loosen the skin over the breast and thighs by gently sliding your fingers underneath.
2. **Season the Turkey:**
   - In a small bowl, mix the butter, olive oil, smoked paprika, garlic powder, onion powder, thyme, cumin, sage, salt, and pepper. Rub the mixture generously over the turkey, both under and over the skin. Stuff the cavity with the lemon, onion, and rosemary.
3. **Roast the Turkey:**
   - Place the turkey on a roasting rack in a large roasting pan. Roast for about 15 minutes per pound, basting every 30 minutes with pan juices. The turkey is done when the in-

ternal temperature reaches 165°F (74°C) in the thickest part of the breast and 175°F (80°C) in the thigh.

4. **Make the Gravy:**
   ◦ While the turkey rests (for about 20 minutes), make the gravy. Melt the butter in a saucepan over medium heat. Whisk in the flour and cook for 1–2 minutes, stirring constantly. Gradually add the turkey drippings or broth, whisking until smooth. Simmer until thickened, then season with salt and pepper.

5. **Serve with All the Fixings:**
   ◦ Carve the turkey and serve with classic sides like stuffing, mashed potatoes, cranberry sauce, and green beans.

The Sand-Seared Turkey with All the Fixings is a flavorful, tender dish that combines tradition with bold, earthy flavors, making it a perfect centerpiece for any holiday celebration.

Festive Graboid Feasts: A Celebration of Flavor

The holidays are a time for gathering, sharing, and indulging in delicious food, and **Festive Graboid Feasts** brings that spirit to life with bold, memorable recipes. The **Holiday Underground Ham** offers a sweet and savory twist on a classic dish, while the **Sand-Seared Turkey with All the Fixings** combines tradition with bold seasoning and mouthwatering sides.

Whether you're hosting a grand holiday dinner or preparing a special meal for your loved ones, these recipes ensure that your table will be filled with warmth, joy, and unforgettable flavors. Celebrate the season with these Graboid-inspired festive dishes and make your holidays truly extraordinary.

Chapter 21: Digging for Gold – Decadent Sides

A feast isn't complete without side dishes that shine as brightly as the main course. **Digging for Gold – Decadent Sides** presents two luxurious recipes that elevate classic comfort foods to new heights. These golden, indulgent dishes are inspired by the earthy richness of the Graboids' underground world and their love for unearthing hidden treasures.

The **Golden Mashed Potatoes with Brown Butter** transform a traditional side into a velvety, nutty delight, while the **Underground Mac 'n' Cheese** combines layers of creamy, cheesy goodness with a golden breadcrumb topping. Perfect for any gathering, these sides are guaranteed to steal the spotlight.

Golden Mashed Potatoes with Brown Butter

Mashed potatoes are a quintessential side dish, but this recipe takes them to the next level with the addition of nutty brown butter, which infuses the potatoes with a rich, golden flavor. These potatoes are creamy, smooth, and luxurious—an ideal pairing for any main course.

Ingredients:

- 3 lbs Yukon Gold potatoes, peeled and cut into chunks
- 1 cup unsalted butter
- ½ cup heavy cream (warm)
- ½ cup whole milk (warm)
- 1 tsp garlic powder
- Salt and pepper to taste
- Optional garnish: chopped fresh chives or parsley

Instructions:

1. **Cook the Potatoes:**
   - Place the potato chunks in a large pot and cover with cold water. Add a generous pinch of salt. Bring to a boil over medium-high heat, then reduce to a simmer. Cook for 15–20 minutes, or until the potatoes are fork-tender.
2. **Prepare the Brown Butter:**
   - While the potatoes are cooking, melt the butter in a small saucepan over medium heat. Swirl the pan occasionally and cook until the butter turns golden brown and develops a nutty aroma, about 5–7 minutes. Remove from heat and set aside.
3. **Mash the Potatoes:**
   - Drain the cooked potatoes and return them to the pot. Mash them using a potato masher or ricer until smooth.

4. **Combine Ingredients:**
   - Gradually add the warm cream, milk, and brown butter to the mashed potatoes, stirring gently until incorporated. Season with garlic powder, salt, and pepper to taste.
5. **Serve and Garnish:**
   - Transfer the mashed potatoes to a serving dish and drizzle with any remaining brown butter. Garnish with chopped chives or parsley, if desired.

Golden Mashed Potatoes with Brown Butter are a decadent, velvety side dish that complements everything from roasted meats to hearty casseroles.

Underground Mac 'n' Cheese

This baked mac 'n' cheese is the epitome of comfort food, featuring a creamy, cheesy sauce and a crispy golden breadcrumb topping. With layers of flavor and texture, it's a dish that will have everyone digging in for seconds.

Ingredients:

For the Mac 'n' Cheese:

- 1 lb elbow macaroni or shell pasta
- 4 tbsp unsalted butter
- 4 tbsp all-purpose flour
- 3 cups whole milk (warm)
- 1 cup heavy cream (warm)
- 2 cups shredded sharp cheddar cheese
- 1 cup shredded Gruyère cheese
- ½ cup grated Parmesan cheese
- 1 tsp Dijon mustard
- ½ tsp smoked paprika
- Salt and pepper to taste

For the Topping:

- 1 cup panko breadcrumbs
- 2 tbsp unsalted butter, melted
- ¼ cup grated Parmesan cheese
- 1 tsp dried parsley (optional)

Instructions:

1. **Cook the Pasta:**
   - Bring a large pot of salted water to a boil. Cook the pasta according to package instructions until al dente. Drain and set aside.
2. **Make the Cheese Sauce:**
   - In a large saucepan, melt the butter over medium heat. Whisk in the flour and cook for 1–2 minutes, stirring constantly, until lightly golden. Gradually whisk in the warm milk and cream, ensuring there are no lumps. Cook for 3–4 minutes, or until the sauce thickens.
   - Stir in the cheddar, Gruyère, and Parmesan cheeses until melted and smooth. Add the Dijon mustard, smoked paprika, salt, and pepper to taste.
3. **Combine and Transfer:**
   - Add the cooked pasta to the cheese sauce, stirring to coat evenly. Transfer the mixture to a greased 9x13-inch baking dish.
4. **Prepare the Topping:**
   - In a small bowl, combine the panko breadcrumbs, melted butter, Parmesan cheese, and parsley. Sprinkle the topping evenly over the mac 'n' cheese.
5. **Bake to Perfection:**
   - Preheat your oven to 375°F (190°C). Bake the mac 'n' cheese for 20–25 minutes, or until the topping is golden brown and crispy.
6. **Serve and Enjoy:**
   - Let the dish cool slightly before serving. Pair with your favorite main course for a truly comforting meal.

Underground Mac 'n' Cheese is a crowd-pleaser with its creamy interior and golden, crunchy topping, making it a perfect addition to any feast.

Digging for Gold: Decadent Sides Worth Celebrating

Side dishes don't have to be an afterthought—they can be the stars of the table. The **Golden Mashed Potatoes with Brown Butter** and **Underground Mac 'n' Cheese** bring luxurious flavors and textures that elevate any meal to a celebration.

These recipes combine comfort and decadence, offering the perfect balance of richness and warmth. Whether for a holiday gathering, a special occasion, or a cozy family dinner, these sides will leave everyone feeling satisfied and eager for more. Dig in and unearth the golden treasures of these unforgettable dishes!

Chapter 22: Subterranean Snacks

When hunger strikes between meals, snacks inspired by the rugged, resourceful world of *Tremors* are the perfect solution. **Subterranean Snacks** offers easy-to-make, portable options that are ideal for adventures, whether you're hiking, working, or just enjoying a cozy day at home.

The **Tremor Trail Mix** combines sweet, salty, and crunchy elements in a mix that's as dynamic as the Graboids themselves. Meanwhile, the **Graboid Granola Bars** are hearty, flavorful, and packed with nutrients, offering a satisfying bite that keeps energy levels high. These snacks are perfect for Graboid-themed parties, prepping for outdoor excursions, or simply indulging in a fun, flavorful treat.

Tremor Trail Mix

This trail mix is a Graboid-inspired medley of nuts, dried fruits, chocolate, and savory snacks that deliver the perfect combination of textures and flavors. It's an easy, customizable snack that's ready in minutes and perfect for on-the-go munching.

Ingredients:

- 1 cup roasted almonds
- 1 cup cashews
- 1 cup pretzel twists or sticks
- ½ cup dried cranberries
- ½ cup golden raisins
- ½ cup dark chocolate chunks or M&Ms
- ½ cup sunflower seeds (hulled)
- 1 tsp smoked paprika or chili powder (optional, for a savory twist)

Instructions:

1. **Combine the Ingredients:**
   - In a large bowl, combine the almonds, cashews, pretzels, dried cranberries, golden raisins, chocolate chunks, and sunflower seeds. Toss to mix evenly.
2. **Add Optional Seasoning:**
   - If you prefer a savory twist, sprinkle smoked paprika or chili powder over the mix and toss again to coat lightly.
3. **Store and Serve:**
   - Divide the trail mix into individual portions using small resealable bags or airtight containers for easy storage.
4. **Enjoy the Adventure:**
   - Keep the trail mix on hand for a quick snack during hikes, road trips, or busy days.

    Tremor Trail Mix is a versatile, nutrient-packed snack that's perfect for fueling any adventure or satisfying mid-day cravings.

Graboid Granola Bars

These granola bars are hearty, chewy, and packed with ingredients that deliver energy and flavor. Inspired by the Graboids' resourcefulness, this recipe uses pantry staples to create a snack that's portable, delicious, and easy to make.

Ingredients:

- 2 cups rolled oats
- ½ cup chopped almonds or pecans
- ½ cup honey or maple syrup
- ½ cup creamy peanut butter or almond butter
- ¼ cup brown sugar
- 1 tsp vanilla extract
- ½ cup dried fruit (e.g., cranberries, raisins, or chopped apricots)
- ½ cup mini chocolate chips or dark chocolate chunks
- ¼ tsp cinnamon
- ¼ tsp salt

Instructions:

1. **Toast the Oats and Nuts (Optional):**
   - Preheat your oven to 350°F (175°C). Spread the oats and chopped almonds or pecans on a baking sheet and toast for 8–10 minutes, stirring once, until lightly golden. Let cool.
2. **Prepare the Wet Mixture:**
   - In a small saucepan, combine the honey or maple syrup, peanut butter, and brown sugar. Heat over low heat, stirring constantly, until the mixture is smooth and well combined. Remove from heat and stir in the vanilla extract.
3. **Mix the Ingredients:**
   - In a large mixing bowl, combine the toasted oats and nuts, dried fruit, chocolate chips, cinnamon, and salt. Pour the warm peanut butter mixture over the dry ingredients and mix well until everything is evenly coated.
4. **Press and Chill:**
   - Line an 8x8-inch baking pan with parchment paper, leaving an overhang for easy removal. Transfer the granola mixture to the pan and press firmly into an even layer. Use the back of a spatula or the bottom of a measuring cup to compact the mixture.
5. **Chill and Set:**
   - Refrigerate the pan for at least 2 hours, or until the granola is firm and set.

6. **Cut and Store:**
   - Remove the granola from the pan using the parchment paper overhang and cut into bars or squares. Store in an airtight container at room temperature or in the refrigerator for up to a week.

The Graboid Granola Bars are a satisfying, portable snack that's perfect for busy days, outdoor adventures, or as a grab-and-go breakfast option.

Subterranean Snacks: Satisfying and Portable

Snacks should be more than just fillers—they should be flavorful, satisfying, and easy to take with you on any adventure. The **Tremor Trail Mix** and **Graboid Granola Bars** deliver on all fronts, offering a mix of sweet, salty, and hearty ingredients that keep hunger at bay.

Whether you're digging into a busy day or exploring the great outdoors, these **Subterranean Snacks** ensure you're fueled and ready for whatever comes your way. Dig in, savor the flavors, and keep the energy flowing!

Chapter 23: Extreme Eating Challenges

For those who crave not just great food but a culinary adventure, **Extreme Eating Challenges** offers dishes that combine bold flavors with an element of fun competition. These recipes are designed for daring eaters and adventurous hosts looking to add some excitement to their gatherings.

The **Tremor Hot Wings Challenge** takes spice to a whole new level, with fiery, flavor-packed wings that will test even the bravest taste buds. Meanwhile, the **Buried Treasure Nachos** deliver layers of gooey, crunchy, and savory goodness, hiding secret ingredients that challenge diners to unearth every hidden treasure. Whether you're hosting a party or looking to shake things up at the dinner table, these dishes are guaranteed to ignite excitement.

Tremor Hot Wings Challenge

This dish is not for the faint of heart! These wings are coated in a fiery hot sauce blend that brings heat, flavor, and a bit of sweat. Perfect for friendly competition or just spicing up your menu, the **Tremor Hot Wings Challenge** will leave diners with a delicious burn and a sense of accomplishment.

Ingredients:

For the Wings:

- 3 lbs chicken wings, split into flats and drumettes
- 2 tbsp vegetable oil
- 1 tsp garlic powder
- 1 tsp onion powder
- 1 tsp smoked paprika
- ½ tsp salt
- ½ tsp black pepper

For the Sauce:

- 1 cup hot sauce (e.g., Frank's RedHot or a super-spicy variant for extra heat)
- 3 tbsp butter
- 1 tbsp honey
- 1 tsp cayenne pepper
- ½ tsp ghost pepper powder (optional, for extreme heat)

Instructions:

1. **Prepare the Wings:**
   - Preheat your oven to 400°F (200°C) or heat your grill to medium-high. Toss the chicken wings with vegetable oil, garlic powder, onion powder, smoked paprika, salt, and pepper until evenly coated.
2. **Cook the Wings:**
   - Arrange the wings in a single layer on a baking sheet lined with foil or a wire rack. Bake for 40–45 minutes, flipping halfway through, until the wings are golden and crispy. If grilling, cook for 15–20 minutes, flipping frequently.
3. **Make the Sauce:**
   - In a small saucepan, combine the hot sauce, butter, honey, cayenne pepper, and ghost pepper powder (if using). Heat over low heat, stirring until the butter is melted and the ingredients are well combined.
4. **Toss the Wings:**
   - Transfer the cooked wings to a large bowl. Pour the hot sauce mixture over the wings and toss until they are evenly coated.
5. **Serve and Challenge:**
   - Plate the wings with celery sticks and a cooling ranch or blue cheese dip on the side. Challenge diners to eat as many wings as they can without reaching for the dip!

The Tremor Hot Wings Challenge is a fiery, flavor-packed experience that will leave guests talking (and maybe crying!) long after the meal is over.

Buried Treasure Nachos

Nachos are a crowd-pleaser, but this version takes it to the next level by layering hidden ingredients throughout the dish. Diners are challenged to find every "buried treasure" while enjoying the gooey, crunchy goodness of loaded nachos.

Ingredients:

For the Base:

- 1 bag tortilla chips (about 12 oz)
- 2 cups shredded cheddar cheese
- 2 cups shredded Monterey Jack cheese

For the Toppings:

- 1 cup seasoned ground beef or shredded chicken
- ½ cup black beans
- ½ cup diced tomatoes
- ¼ cup sliced jalapeños
- ½ cup guacamole (hidden under a layer of chips)
- ½ cup sour cream (hidden under a layer of cheese)
- ½ cup diced pineapple or mango (optional, for a sweet twist)
- ¼ cup chopped green onions

Instructions:

1. **Prepare the Base Layer:**
   - Preheat your oven to 375°F (190°C). Spread half of the tortilla chips on a large baking sheet or oven-safe platter.
2. **Layer the Treasures:**
   - Scatter half of the cheddar and Monterey Jack cheeses over the chips. Add half of the ground beef or chicken, black beans, and diced tomatoes. Hide spoonfuls of guacamole and sour cream under a layer of chips. If using pineapple or mango, scatter small amounts throughout for a sweet surprise.
3. **Add the Second Layer:**
   - Add another layer of chips, followed by the remaining cheese, meat, black beans, and tomatoes. Top with sliced jalapeños and a sprinkle of green onions.
4. **Bake the Nachos:**
   - Bake for 10–12 minutes, or until the cheese is melted and bubbly.
5. **Serve and Challenge:**
   - Serve the nachos hot and challenge diners to find all the "buried treasures." Provide small prizes for those who uncover every hidden ingredient!

The Buried Treasure Nachos are a fun, interactive dish that combines the joy of discovery with the deliciousness of loaded nachos.

Extreme Eating Challenges: Food and Fun

Food isn't just about flavor—it's about experience, and **Extreme Eating Challenges** brings excitement and adventure to the table. The **Tremor Hot Wings Challenge** pushes the boundaries of spice, while the **Buried Treasure Nachos** turn a classic dish into a fun, interactive game.

Whether you're hosting a party or just looking to shake up your dinner routine, these recipes ensure your meal is as entertaining as it is delicious. Prepare for laughter, excitement, and full stomachs as you tackle these bold challenges!

Chapter 24: Kids' Kitchen Adventures

Cooking with kids can be a delightful and rewarding experience, sparking their creativity while introducing them to the joys of food. **Kids' Kitchen Adventures** features recipes designed to engage little ones in the kitchen while keeping things simple, fun, and delicious. These dishes are inspired by the playful spirit of *Tremors* and offer hands-on activities that make cooking a memorable adventure.

The **Mini Tremor Pizzas** allow kids to customize their own personal pizzas with creative toppings, while the **Sand Trap Dirt Pudding Cups** are a whimsical dessert that combines layers of pudding, cookies, and candy for a sweet treat that looks as fun as it tastes. Perfect for family cooking sessions, parties, or rainy-day activities, these recipes make the kitchen a playground for culinary creativity.

Mini Tremor Pizzas

These personal-sized pizzas are a fun, customizable meal that lets kids experiment with toppings and shapes. The process of assembling their own pizzas makes it an interactive and rewarding experience, with delicious results.

Ingredients (makes 6 mini pizzas):

- 1 lb pizza dough (store-bought or homemade)
- ½ cup pizza sauce
- 2 cups shredded mozzarella cheese
- Assorted toppings (pepperoni, diced bell peppers, sliced olives, mushrooms, pineapple chunks, etc.)
- 2 tbsp olive oil
- Optional garnish: fresh basil or oregano

Instructions:

1. **Prepare the Dough:**
   - Preheat your oven to 450°F (230°C) and line a baking sheet with parchment paper. Divide the pizza dough into 6 equal portions and roll each into a small circle or desired shape (e.g., ovals, hearts, or Graboid-inspired squiggles).
2. **Add the Sauce:**
   - Spread a spoonful of pizza sauce onto each dough portion, leaving a small border around the edges.
3. **Layer the Cheese:**
   - Sprinkle a generous amount of shredded mozzarella cheese over the sauce.
4. **Customize the Toppings:**
   - Let kids add their favorite toppings, creating fun patterns or themes. Encourage creativity—maybe a Graboid face with olive eyes and pepperoni mouth or a "sand landscape" with diced veggies!
5. **Bake the Pizzas:**
   - Brush the edges of the dough with olive oil for a golden crust. Bake for 8–10 minutes, or until the cheese is bubbly and the crust is golden brown.
6. **Serve and Enjoy:**
   - Let the pizzas cool slightly before serving. Garnish with fresh basil or oregano for an extra touch of flavor.

Mini Tremor Pizzas are a hands-on, tasty way to get kids excited about cooking and eating their creations.

Sand Trap Dirt Pudding Cups

This whimsical dessert combines layers of chocolate pudding, crushed cookies, and candy "treasures" to create a sweet treat that looks like a sandy Graboid trap. Easy to assemble and endlessly customizable, it's a surefire hit with kids and adults alike.

Ingredients (makes 6 cups):

- 2 cups chocolate pudding (store-bought or homemade)
- 1 cup crushed chocolate sandwich cookies (e.g., Oreos)
- 6 gummy worms or candy snakes
- ½ cup candy "treasures" (e.g., chocolate rocks, gold foil-wrapped coins, or candy pearls)
- 6 clear plastic cups
- Optional toppings: whipped cream or sprinkles

Instructions:

1. **Prepare the Cups:**
   - Place a thin layer of crushed cookies at the bottom of each cup to create the "sand trap" base.
2. **Layer the Pudding:**
   - Spoon chocolate pudding into each cup, filling halfway. Sprinkle another layer of crushed cookies over the pudding.
3. **Hide the Treasures:**
   - Add candy treasures, such as chocolate rocks or gold coins, on top of the cookie layer. Cover with more pudding, filling the cups almost to the top.
4. **Top with Dirt and Worms:**
   - Sprinkle a final layer of crushed cookies over the top. Add gummy worms or candy snakes, letting them peek out for a playful effect.
5. **Optional Garnishes:**
   - Add whipped cream or sprinkles for extra flair.
6. **Serve and Enjoy:**
   - Hand out spoons and let the kids dig into their Sand Trap Dirt Pudding Cups to discover the hidden treasures.

This fun and interactive dessert is perfect for parties, playdates, or family movie nights with a *Tremors* theme.

Kids' Kitchen Adventures: Fun, Flavor, and Creativity

Cooking with kids is about more than just making food—it's about creating memories and encouraging creativity. The **Mini Tremor Pizzas** and **Sand Trap Dirt Pudding Cups** turn the kitchen into an adventure zone, where young chefs can express themselves and have fun.

These recipes are simple enough for little hands to help but deliver big on flavor and excitement. Whether for a special occasion or a casual family day, these dishes ensure that everyone has a great time cooking—and eating—together. Dig in and let the culinary adventures begin!

Chapter 25: Feeding the Horde – Party Platters

When hosting a crowd, presentation and variety are key. **Feeding the Horde – Party Platters** focuses on creating visually stunning and delicious spreads that cater to a variety of tastes while tying into the *Tremors* theme. These platters are designed to impress your guests, combining creativity, flavor, and fun for unforgettable gatherings.

The **Underground Charcuterie Board** is a feast for the senses, featuring a mix of savory meats, cheeses, fruits, and snacks arranged with earthy, Graboid-inspired flair. Meanwhile, the **Graboid-Themed Cupcake Tower** is a towering dessert centerpiece that adds a playful and delicious touch to any event.

Underground Charcuterie Board

A charcuterie board is more than just a snack platter—it's a culinary work of art. This version draws inspiration from the Graboids' subterranean world, incorporating earthy tones, varied textures, and bold flavors for a truly memorable presentation.

Ingredients (suggestions):

Proteins:

- Sliced salami
- Prosciutto
- Smoked turkey or ham
- Spicy chorizo or pepperoni

Cheeses:

- Sharp cheddar
- Brie or camembert
- Gouda (smoked or aged)
- Blue cheese or gorgonzola

Fruits and Vegetables:

- Dried apricots or figs
- Fresh grapes or apple slices
- Cherry tomatoes
- Pickles or olives

Crackers and Breads:

- Artisan crackers
- Crostini or baguette slices
- Pretzel twists

Extras:

- Honeycomb or small jar of honey
- Spicy mustard or savory spreads
- Nuts (e.g., almonds, walnuts, or pistachios)
- Dark chocolate chunks (optional, for contrast)

Instructions:

1. **Choose Your Board:**
   - Select a large wooden or slate board to serve as the base. The natural material enhances the earthy, underground aesthetic.
2. **Arrange the Proteins and Cheeses:**
   - Start with the sliced meats and cheeses, placing them in different sections of the board. Roll or fold the meats into decorative shapes for visual appeal.
3. **Add Fruits and Vegetables:**
   - Scatter the fruits, tomatoes, pickles, and olives around the board, filling in gaps and adding pops of color.
4. **Include Crackers and Breads:**
   - Arrange the crackers, crostini, or baguette slices in neat stacks or overlapping rows for easy access.
5. **Finish with Extras:**
   - Add small bowls or ramekins of honey, mustard, or spreads. Scatter nuts and chocolate chunks for added texture and flavor contrast.
6. **Serve and Enjoy:**
   - Place the charcuterie board at the center of your table and let guests graze freely. Pair with wine, sparkling water, or cocktails for the ultimate party experience.

The Underground Charcuterie Board is a versatile and visually stunning platter that will keep your guests coming back for more.

Graboid-Themed Cupcake Tower

This towering dessert display is as playful as it is delicious. Featuring cupcakes decorated with Graboid-inspired designs and layered on a multi-tiered stand, it's a show-stopping centerpiece for any *Tremors*-themed gathering.

Ingredients (makes 24 cupcakes):

For the Cupcakes:

- 2 ½ cups all-purpose flour
- 1 ¾ cups granulated sugar
- 1 tsp baking powder
- ½ tsp baking soda
- ½ tsp salt
- 1 cup unsalted butter (softened)
- 4 large eggs
- 1 cup whole milk
- 2 tsp vanilla extract

For the Frosting:

- 1 cup unsalted butter (softened)
- 4 cups powdered sugar
- 2 tsp vanilla extract
- 2–3 tbsp heavy cream or milk
- Food coloring (black, gray, brown, and red)

For Decorations:

- Crushed chocolate cookies (for "dirt")
- Gummy worms or candy snakes
- Chocolate shards (for "rocks")
- Piping bags and tips

Instructions:

1. **Bake the Cupcakes:**
   - Preheat your oven to 350°F (175°C) and line two 12-cup muffin tins with paper liners.
   - In a large bowl, mix the flour, sugar, baking powder, baking soda, and salt. Add the butter, eggs, milk, and vanilla extract, and beat until smooth.
   - Divide the batter evenly among the liners and bake for 18–20 minutes, or until a toothpick inserted in the center comes out clean. Let cool completely.
2. **Prepare the Frosting:**
   - Beat the butter until creamy, then gradually add the powdered sugar. Mix in the vanilla extract and heavy cream until the frosting reaches a spreadable consistency. Divide the frosting into bowls and tint with food coloring to create black, gray, brown, and red.
3. **Decorate the Cupcakes:**
   - Frost the cupcakes using piping bags or an offset spatula. Use black and gray for Graboid "bodies," brown for "dirt," and red for "blood" accents.
   - Sprinkle crushed cookies on some cupcakes for a dirt effect, and add gummy worms, candy snakes, or chocolate shards for fun, Graboid-themed details.
4. **Assemble the Tower:**
   - Arrange the decorated cupcakes on a multi-tiered cupcake stand, starting with larger cupcakes on the bottom and smaller ones on top for a pyramid effect.
5. **Serve and Wow Your Guests:**
   - Place the cupcake tower in a prominent spot and let guests marvel at the creative designs before digging in.

The Graboid-Themed Cupcake Tower is a playful and delicious dessert display that's sure to be the highlight of any party.

Feeding the Horde: A Feast for the Eyes and Palate

Party platters are all about variety, presentation, and crowd-pleasing flavors, and **Feeding the Horde – Party Platters** delivers on all fronts. The **Underground Charcuterie Board** offers a savory, shareable spread, while the **Graboid-Themed Cupcake Tower** adds a sweet, whimsical touch to your gathering.

These platters make hosting easy and fun, giving your guests an unforgettable culinary experience while celebrating the adventurous spirit of *Tremors*. Dig in, share the joy, and let the feasting begin!

Appendix A: Ingredient Substitutions

Cooking is an art that thrives on flexibility, and having alternatives for dietary needs or hard-to-find ingredients can make any recipe more accessible. **Appendix A: Ingredient Substitutions** provides a comprehensive guide for adapting recipes without sacrificing flavor or quality. Whether you're catering to dietary restrictions, facing ingredient shortages, or simply looking for creative swaps, this guide ensures you can still enjoy the full range of flavors from the recipes in this book.

Tips for Adapting Recipes for Dietary Restrictions

1. **Gluten-Free Adaptations:**
   - Replace all-purpose flour with a gluten-free flour blend (e.g., Bob's Red Mill or King Arthur Baking). These blends often work cup-for-cup in baking and cooking.
   - Use gluten-free breadcrumbs or crushed rice crackers in recipes like meatballs, breaded dishes, or toppings.
   - Opt for gluten-free pasta in dishes like mac 'n' cheese or lasagna.

2. **Dairy-Free Options:**
   - Replace butter with plant-based alternatives like Earth Balance or coconut oil (note that coconut oil may add a slight coconut flavor).
   - Use almond, soy, oat, or coconut milk instead of whole milk or cream in soups, sauces, and baked goods.
   - Swap dairy-based cheese for plant-based cheeses like those from Daiya or Violife.

3. **Vegetarian and Vegan Adaptations:**
   - Replace meat with tofu, tempeh, seitan, or legumes (e.g., lentils, chickpeas, or black beans) in recipes like chili, casseroles, or stir-fries.
   - Substitute eggs with flaxseed or chia seeds (1 tbsp flax/chia + 3 tbsp water = 1 egg) in baking.
   - Use nutritional yeast instead of Parmesan cheese for a cheesy flavor in pasta and sauces.

4. **Low-Sodium Adjustments:**
   - Use low-sodium or unsalted versions of broth, soy sauce, and canned goods.
   - Season with herbs, spices, and citrus instead of extra salt to enhance flavor.

5. **Low-Carb/Keto Options:**
   - Replace rice or pasta with cauliflower rice or zucchini noodles in casseroles or stir-fries.
   - Use almond flour or coconut flour instead of wheat flour for baking or breading.

6. **Nut-Free Substitutions:**
   - Replace almond or peanut butter with sunflower seed butter in sauces, desserts, or snacks.
   - Use toasted seeds (e.g., pumpkin or sunflower seeds) instead of nuts in salads or granola.

7. **Sugar-Free Adjustments:**
   - Substitute white sugar with natural sweeteners like stevia, monk fruit, or erythritol for a low-glycemic option.

◦ Use unsweetened applesauce or mashed bananas as natural sweeteners in baked goods.

Alternative Ingredients for Hard-to-Find Items

1. **Spices and Seasonings:**
   - ◦ **Smoked paprika:** Replace with a mix of regular paprika and a pinch of cumin for a smoky flavor.
   - ◦ **Curry paste:** Use curry powder mixed with a small amount of water or coconut milk.
   - ◦ **Ground coriander:** Swap with a mix of ground cumin and lemon zest for a similar flavor profile.
2. **Dairy Products:**
   - ◦ **Buttermilk:** Substitute 1 cup of buttermilk with 1 cup of milk and 1 tbsp of vinegar or lemon juice; let sit for 5 minutes.
   - ◦ **Heavy cream:** Use equal parts milk and melted butter, or substitute with coconut cream for a dairy-free option.
3. **Meats and Proteins:**
   - ◦ **Ground beef:** Replace with ground turkey, chicken, or plant-based ground meat (e.g., Beyond Meat or Impossible Burger).
   - ◦ **Bacon:** Use turkey bacon or smoked tempeh for a leaner or plant-based alternative.
   - ◦ **Seafood:** Swap shrimp with diced chicken or firm tofu, or use canned tuna/salmon in recipes that call for fresh fish.
4. **Sweeteners:**
   - ◦ **Honey:** Replace with maple syrup, agave nectar, or a simple syrup made with sugar and water.
   - ◦ **Molasses:** Use dark brown sugar, maple syrup, or honey for similar depth and sweetness.
5. **Flours and Grains:**
   - ◦ **All-purpose flour:** Use whole wheat flour for a heartier texture or almond/coconut flour for gluten-free recipes.
   - ◦ **Rice:** Substitute with quinoa, farro, or couscous depending on the desired texture and flavor.
6. **Cheeses:**
   - ◦ **Ricotta cheese:** Replace with cottage cheese blended until smooth or use silken tofu for a vegan alternative.
   - ◦ **Parmesan cheese:** Swap with Pecorino Romano or nutritional yeast for a dairy-free option.
7. **Vegetables and Fruits:**
   - ◦ **Bell peppers:** Use zucchini, eggplant, or mushrooms for similar texture and versatility.
   - ◦ **Fresh herbs:** Replace fresh herbs with dried (use one-third the amount of fresh) or mix dried herbs with a splash of lemon juice for freshness.

8. **Specialty Items:**
   - **Tahini:** Use almond butter or peanut butter thinned with a little water or oil.
   - **Coconut milk:** Substitute with heavy cream, half-and-half, or a mix of milk and unsweetened shredded coconut.
   - **Miso paste:** Use a small amount of soy sauce or fish sauce to replicate the salty umami flavor.

Closing Notes

With these substitution tips, you can adapt the recipes in this book to suit almost any dietary restriction or ingredient limitation. Cooking is all about creativity, and these swaps allow you to maintain flavor and texture while accommodating your needs. Experiment, have fun, and remember—there's always a way to make the dish work!

Appendix B: Cooking Tips and Techniques

Mastering the art of cooking is about more than just following recipes—it's about understanding the techniques that bring out the best in your ingredients. **Appendix B: Cooking Tips and Techniques** provides insights into two key skills that enhance the subterranean theme of this book: slow cooking for deep, earthy flavors and creating the visual and textural "burrowed" effects that give dishes a unique, Graboid-inspired twist.

How to Perfect Slow Cooking for Underground Flavors

Slow cooking is the ideal method for developing rich, deep flavors reminiscent of meals cooked beneath the earth's surface. It allows spices to bloom, proteins to tenderize, and ingredients to meld into harmonious dishes. Here's how to master this technique:

1. **Choosing the Right Equipment:**
   - Use a slow cooker, Dutch oven, or heavy-bottomed pot. These vessels retain heat evenly, ensuring consistent cooking over long periods.
2. **Layering Ingredients:**
   - Place dense ingredients like root vegetables (potatoes, carrots, parsnips) at the bottom, as they take longer to cook. Add proteins, liquids, and delicate vegetables in layers to ensure everything cooks evenly.
3. **Browning for Depth:**
   - Searing meats and aromatics (like onions, garlic, and spices) before slow cooking adds a caramelized, umami-rich base to your dishes. While optional, this step significantly enhances flavor.
4. **Balancing Liquids:**
   - Slow cooking doesn't require much liquid because moisture doesn't evaporate as it would with other cooking methods. Use just enough to cover the ingredients—overdoing it can result in diluted flavors.
5. **Using Herbs and Spices:**
   - Add dried herbs and spices early in the cooking process to allow their flavors to develop fully. For fresh herbs, add them toward the end to maintain their brightness.
6. **Low and Slow:**
   - Cook on low heat whenever possible to give the flavors time to develop. Most recipes take 6–8 hours on low or 3–4 hours on high, but the slower, the better for optimal results.
7. **Avoid Overstirring:**
   - Resist the urge to frequently lift the lid and stir. Every time you do, heat escapes, lengthening cooking time and potentially disturbing the natural layering of flavors.
8. **Finishing Touches:**
   - Adjust seasoning at the end of cooking. A splash of vinegar, a pinch of salt, or a sprinkle of fresh herbs can brighten the flavors of long-simmered dishes.

Secrets to Creating the Ultimate "Burrowed" Effect in Dishes

The burrowed effect ties directly into the *Tremors* theme, creating dishes that mimic the texture and appearance of Graboids' underground tunnels. Here's how to achieve it in a variety of recipes:

1. **Layering Techniques for Visual Depth:**
   - In casseroles or baked dishes, create multiple layers of contrasting colors and textures (e.g., cheese, sauces, and vegetables) to evoke a burrowed look.
   - For desserts like dirt pudding cups, use crushed cookies, pudding, and candy layers to resemble underground strata.

2. **Using Textural Contrasts:**
   - Combine smooth and crunchy elements, such as creamy fillings and crispy toppings, to mimic the uneven textures of an underground burrow.
   - Incorporate crushed nuts, breadcrumbs, or toasted grains to add a tactile "gritty" effect.

3. **Edible "Soil" and "Rocks":**
   - Use crushed cookies, cocoa powder, or ground coffee to create edible "soil" in savory or sweet dishes.
   - Incorporate chocolate rocks, candied nuts, or toasted seeds for a fun geological touch.

4. **Creating Tunnels and Cavities:**
   - In baked goods like cupcakes or cakes, carve small cavities and fill them with hidden surprises (e.g., fruit compote, chocolate ganache, or candy) to replicate burrowed tunnels.
   - Use a piping bag to inject fillings into donuts, muffins, or eclairs for a fun, hidden "burrow" effect.

5. **Swirling and Marbling:**
   - In dishes like lasagna or mac 'n' cheese, swirl sauces or layer them unevenly to mimic the natural, chaotic look of underground formations.
   - For desserts, marble batters or frostings to create visual depth and intrigue.

6. **Shaping and Plating:**
   - Shape doughs or mold ingredients into curves, spirals, or organic patterns to evoke the movement of a burrowing creature.
   - Plate dishes with scattered garnishes and asymmetrical arrangements to mirror the randomness of an underground habitat.

7. **Incorporating Natural Colors:**
   - Use earthy tones like browns, greens, and dark reds in your ingredients. Beet juice, spinach, turmeric, and cocoa powder can add natural colors to dishes.
   - Highlight contrasts with vibrant accents like fresh herbs, edible flowers, or brightly colored vegetables.

Closing Notes

Cooking is as much about presentation and experience as it is about flavor. By mastering slow cooking, you can create rich, earthy dishes that embody underground flavors, while the burrowed effect adds a touch of creativity and fun to your meals.

Use these tips and techniques to elevate your cooking, whether you're making a rustic family dinner or an elaborate *Tremors*-themed feast. The result will be dishes that look as stunning as they taste, delighting the eyes and the palate alike.

Conclusion: Unearthing Culinary Creativity

As we reach the end of this culinary adventure, it's time to reflect on the creativity, bold flavors, and fun that have brought the spirit of the Graboids to life in your kitchen. This cookbook has been a celebration of imaginative cooking, where themes of subterranean survival and *Tremors*-inspired ingenuity meet the universal joy of sharing good food with others.

Celebrating Graboid-Inspired Culinary Creativity

The Graboids may be fictional, but the inspiration they provide is anything but. From crafting hearty meals like **Sand-Seared Turkey** to playful desserts like **Sand Trap Dirt Pudding Cups**, this cookbook has explored how food can tell a story, evoke emotions, and even spark a sense of adventure.

These recipes have pushed boundaries, transforming classic comfort foods into bold creations that capture the essence of the underground world. Whether it was through smoky, slow-cooked dishes, visually striking "burrowed" effects, or daring flavor combinations, this journey has proven that cooking is not just a necessity—it's an art form.

By stepping out of your culinary comfort zone, you've embraced the Graboid ethos: adapt, innovate, and dig deep into the creative potential of your ingredients. Every recipe in this book, whether sweet, savory, or spicy, is a tribute to the adventurous spirit of *Tremors* and the power of food to bring people together.

Encouraging Readers to Share Their Own Graboid-Inspired Recipes

The beauty of cooking lies in its ability to evolve. As you've explored these recipes, you've likely discovered your own twists, substitutions, and ideas. Perhaps your **Underground Mac 'n' Cheese** featured a secret ingredient, or your **Tremor Trail Mix** became a family favorite with a unique blend of snacks. Whatever the case, your creativity has brought these recipes to life in ways only you can.

Now, the challenge is to go further. Experiment with new flavors, textures, and techniques inspired by the Graboids' unpredictable nature. Think about how you can reinterpret classic dishes, add playful twists, or even invent entirely new recipes that align with the underground theme.

We invite you to share your creations with others—whether through social media, community potlucks, or gatherings with family and friends. Use hashtags like **#GraboidEats** or **#TremorsKitchen** to showcase your culinary achievements, connect with fellow fans, and inspire others to dig into the world of Graboid-inspired cuisine.

A Final Toast to Culinary Adventure

Cooking is more than following instructions; it's about exploration, experimentation, and connecting with others through shared meals. This cookbook has been a journey through flavors, creativity, and imagination, and we hope it has inspired you to approach cooking with the same daring spirit as a survivalist in Perfection Valley.

As you continue to cook, remember that every dish tells a story, and every meal is an opportunity to bring joy to those around you. Whether it's a fiery **Tremor Hot Wings Challenge**, a nostalgic **Underground Root Beer Float**, or a show-stopping **Graboid-Themed Cupcake Tower**, let your culinary creations reflect your passion, humor, and ingenuity.

So here's to you, to the Graboids, and to the delicious, adventurous meals yet to come. May your kitchen always be a place of inspiration, laughter, and extraordinary flavors.

Dig in, explore, and keep the spirit of the Graboids alive—one bite at a time.

Bon appétit!

<u>**Message from the Author:**</u>

I hope you enjoyed this book, I love astrology and knew there was not a book such as this out on the shelf. I love metaphysical items as well. Please check out my other books:

-Life of Government Benefits

-My life of Hell

-My life with Hydrocephalus

-Red Sky

-World Domination:Woman's rule

-World Domination:Woman's Rule 2: The War

-Life and Banishment of Apophis: book 1

-The Kidney Friendly Diet

-The Ultimate Hemp Cookbook

-Creating a Dispensary(legally)

-Cleanliness throughout life: the importance of showering from childhood to adulthood.

-Strong Roots: The Risks of Overcoddling children

-Hemp Horoscopes: Cosmic Insights and Earthly Healing

- Celestial Hemp Navigating the Zodiac: Through the Green Cosmos

-Astrological Hemp: Aligning The Stars with Earth's Ancient Herb

-The Astrological Guide to Hemp: Stars, Signs, and Sacred Leaves

-Green Growth: Innovative Marketing Strategies for your Hemp Products and Dispensary

-Cosmic Cannabis

-Astrological Munchies

-Henry The Hemp

-Zodiacal Roots: The Astrological Soul Of Hemp

- Green Constellations: Intersection of Hemp and Zodiac

-Hemp in The Houses: An astrological Adventure Through The Cannabis Galaxy

-Galactic Ganja Guide

Heavenly Hemp

Zodiac Leaves

Doctor Who Astrology

Cannastrology

Stellar Satvias and Cosmic Indicas

<u>Celestial Cannabis: A Zodiac Journey</u>

AstroHerbology: The Sky and The Soil: Volume 1

AstroHerbology:Celestial Cannabis:Volume 2

Cosmic Cannabis Cultivation

The Starry Guide to Herbal Harmony: Volume 1

The Starry Guide to Herbal Harmony: Cannabis Universe: Volume 2

Yugioh Astrology: Astrological Guide to Deck, Duels and more

Nightmare Mansion: Echoes of The Abyss

Nightmare Mansion 2: Legacy of Shadows

Nightmare Mansion 3: Shadows of the Forgotten
Nightmare Mansion 4: Echoes of the Damned
The Life and Banishment of Apophis: Book 2
Nightmare Mansion: Halls of Despair
<u>Healing with Herb: Cannabis and Hydrocephalus</u>
<u>Planetary Pot: Aligning with Astrological Herbs: Volume 1</u>
Fast Track to Freedom: 30 Days to Financial Independence Using AI, Assets, and Agile Hustles
<u>Cosmic Hemp Pathways</u>
How to Become Financially Free in 30 Days: 10,000 Paths to Prosperity
Zodiacal Herbage: Astrological Insights: Volume 1
Nightmare Mansion: Whispers in the Walls
The Daleks Invade Atlantis
Henry the hemp and Hydrocephalus

10X The Kidney Friendly Diet
Cannabis Universe: Adult coloring book
Hemp Astrology: The Healing Power of the Stars
Zodiacal Herbage: Astrological Insights: Cannabis Universe: Volume 2
<u>Planetary Pot: Aligning with Astrological Herbs: Cannabis Universes: Volume 2</u>
Doctor Who Meets the Replicators and SG-1: The Ultimate Battle for Survival
Nightmare Mansion: Curse of the Blood Moon
<u>The Celestial Stoner: A Guide to the Zodiac</u>
Cosmic Pleasures: Sex Toy Astrology for Every Sign
Hydrocephalus Astrology: Navigating the Stars and Healing Waters
Lapis and the Mischievous Chocolate Bar

Celestial Positions: Sexual Astrology for Every Sign
Apophis's Shadow Work Journal: **:** A Journey of Self-Discovery and Healing
Kinky Cosmos: Sexual Kink Astrology for Every Sign
Digital Cosmos: The Astrological Digimon Compendium
Stellar Seeds: The Cosmic Guide to Growing with Astrology
Apophis's Daily Gratitude Journal

Cat Astrology: Feline Mysteries of the Cosmos
The Cosmic Kama Sutra: An Astrological Guide to Sexual Positions
Unleash Your Potential: A Guided Journal Powered by AI Insights
Whispers of the Enchanted Grove

Cosmic Pleasures: An Astrological Guide to Sexual Kinks
369, 12 Manifestation Journal

Whisper of the nocturne journal(blank journal for writing or drawing)
The Boogey Book
Locked In Reflection: A Chastity Journey Through Locktober
Generating Wealth Quickly:
How to Generate $100,000 in 24 Hours
Star Magic: Harness the Power of the Universe
The Flatulence Chronicles: A Fart Journal for Self-Discovery
The Doctor and The Death Moth
Seize the Day: A Personal Seizure Tracking Journal
The Ultimate Boogeyman Safari: A Journey into the Boogie World and Beyond
Whispers of Samhain: 1,000 Spells of Love, Luck, and Lunar Magic: Samhain Spell Book
Apophis's guides:
Witch's Spellbook Crafting Guide for Halloween
<u>Frost & Flame: The Enchanted Yule Grimoire of 1000 Winter Spells</u>
<u>The Ultimate Boogey Goo Guide & Spooky Activities for Halloween Fun</u>
Harmony of the Scales: A Libra's Spellcraft for Balance and Beauty
The Enchanted Advent: 36 Days of Christmas Wonders

Nightmare Mansion: The Labyrinth of Screams
Harvest of Enchantment: 1,000 Spells of Gratitude, Love, and Fortune for Thanksgiving
The Boogey Chronicles: A Journal of Nightly Encounters and Shadowy Secrets
The 12 Days of Financial Freedom: A Step-by-Step Christmas Countdown to Transform Your Finances
Sigil of the Eternal Spiral Blank Journal
A Christmas Feast: Timeless Recipes for Every Meal
Holiday Stress-Free Solutions: A Survival Guide to Thriving During the Festive Season
Yu-Gi-Oh! Holiday Gifting Mastery: The Ultimate Guide for Fans and Newcomers Alike
Holiday Harmony: A Hydrocephalus Survival Guide for the Festive Season
Celestial Craft: The Witch's Almanac for 2025 – A Cosmic Guide to Manifestations, Moons, and Mystical Events
Doctor Who: The Toymaker's Winter Wonderland
Tulsa King Unveiled: A Thrilling Guide to Stallone's Mafia Masterpiece
Pendulum Craft: A Complete Guide to Crafting and Using Personalized Divination Tools
Nightmare Mansion: Santa's Eternal Eve
Starlight Noel: A Cosmic Journey through Christmas Mysteries
The Dark Architect: Unlocking the Blueprint of Existence
Surviving the Embrace: The Ultimate Guide to Encounters with The Hugging Molly
The Enchanted Codex: Secrets of the Craft for Witches, Wiccans, and Pagans
Harvest of Gratitude: A Complete Thanksgiving Guide
Yuletide Essentials: A Complete Guide to an Authentic and Magical Christmas
Celestial Smokes: A Cosmic Guide to Cigars and Astrology

Living in Balance: A Comprehensive Survival Guide to Thriving with Diabetes Insipidus
Cosmic Symbiosis: The Venom Zodiac Chronicles
The Cursed Paw of Ambition
Cosmic Symbiosis: The Astrological Venom Journal
Celestial Wonders Unfold: A Stargazer's Guide to the Cosmos (2024-2029)
The Ultimate Black Friday Prepper's Guide: Mastering Shopping Strategies and Savings
Cosmic Sales: The Astrological Guide to Black Friday Shopping
Legends of the Corn Mother and Other Harvest Myths
Whispers of the Harvest: The Corn Mother's Journal
The Evergreen Spellbook
The Doctor Meets the Boogeyman
The White Witch of Rose Hall's SpellBook
The Gingerbread Golem's Shadow: A Study in Sweet Darkness
The Gingerbread Golem Codex: An Academic Exploration of Sweet Myths
The Gingerbread Golem Grimoire: Sweet Magicks and Spells for the Festive Witch
The Curse of the Gingerbread Golem
10-minute Christmas Crafts for kids
<u>Christmas Crisis Solutions: The Ultimate Last-Minute Survival Guide</u>
Gingerbread Golem Recipes: Holiday Treats with a Magical Twist
The Infinite Key: Unlocking Mystical Secrets of the Ages
Enchanted Yule: A Wiccan and Pagan Guide to a Magical and Memorable Season
Dinosaurs of Power: Unlocking Ancient Magick
Astro-Dinos: The Cosmic Guide to Prehistoric Wisdom
Gallifrey's Yule Logs: A Festive Doctor Who Cookbook
The Dino Grimoire: Secrets of Prehistoric Magick
The Gift They Never Knew They Needed
The Gingerbread Golem's Culinary Alchemy: Enchanting Recipes for a Sweetly Dark Feast
A Time Lord Christmas: Holiday Adventures with the Doctor
Krampusproofing Your Home: Defensive Strategies for Yule
Silent Frights: A Collection of Christmas Creepypastas to Chill Your Bones
Santa Raptor's Jolly Carnage: A Dino-Claus Christmas Tale
Prehistoric Palettes: A Dino Wicca Coloring Journey
The Christmas Wishkeeper Chronicles
The Starlight Sleigh: A Holiday Journey
Elf Secrets: The True Magic of the North Pole
Candy Cane Conjurations
Cooking with Kids: Recipes Under 20 Minutes
Doctor Who: The TARDIS Confiscation
The Anxiety First Aid Kit: Quick Tools to Calm Your Mind
Frosty Whispers: A Winter's Tale
The Infinite Key: Unlocking the Secrets to Prosperity, Resilience, and Purpose

The Grasping Void: Why You'll Regret This Purchase
Astrology for Busy Bees: Star Signs Simplified
The Instant Focus Formula: Cut Through the Noise
The Secret Language of Colors: Unlocking the Emotional Codes
Sacred Fossil Chronicles: Blank Journal
The Christmas Cottage Miracle
If you want solar for your home go here: https://www.harborsolar.live/apophisenterprises/

Get Some Tarot cards: https://www.makeplayingcards.com/sell/apophis-occult-shop

Get some shirts: https://www.bonfire.com/store/apophis-shirt-emporium/

<u>Instagrams:</u>
@apophis_enterprises,
@apophisbookemporium,
@apophisscardshop
Twitter: @apophisenterpr1
Tiktok:@apophisenterprise
Youtube: @sg1fan23477, @FiresideRetreatKingdom
Hive: @sg1fan23477
CheeLee: @SG1fan23477

Podcast: Apophis Chat Zone: https://open.spotify.com/show/5zXbr-CLEV2xzCp8ybrfHsk?si=fb4d4fdbdce44dec

Newsletter: https://apophiss-newsletter-27c897.beehiiv.com/

If you want to support me or see posts of other projects that I have come over to: **buymeacof-fee.com/mpetchinskg**
I post there daily several times a day

Get your Dinowicca or Christmas themed digital products, especially Santa Raptor songs and other musics. Here: **https://sg1fan23477.gumroad.com**

Apophis Yuletide Digital has not only digital Christmas items, but it will have all things with Dinowicca as well as other Digital products.

www.ingramcontent.com/pod-product-compliance
Lightning Source LLC
Chambersburg PA
CBHW080715120726
48001CB00010B/3031